OCT - - 2007

A VIRTUOUS WOMAN

A NOVEL BY KAYE GIBBONS

A · VIRTUOUS

ALGONQUIN BOOKS

OF CHAPEL HILL

1989

· WOMAN

Published by
Algonquin Books of Chapel Hill
Post Office Box 2225
Chapel Hill, North Carolina 27515-2225
a division of
Workman Publishing Company, Inc.
708 Broadway
New York, New York 10003

Design by Molly Renda.

LIBRARY OF CONGRESS CATALOGING-IN-PUBLICATION DATA
        Gibbons, Kaye, 1960–
        A virtuous woman / Kaye Gibbons.
            p. cm.
        ISBN 0-945575-09-2
        I. Title.
        PS 3557.1 13917v57   1989
        813'.54—dc 19   88-22026
                                    CIP
        New ISBN 1-56512-206-2
        10 9 8 7 6 5 4

To Michael

for his extraordinary patience and love

A virtuous woman who can find?
For her price is far above rubies.
The heart of her husband trusteth in her,
And he shall have no lack of gain.
She doeth him good and not evil
All the days of her life.
She seeketh wool and flax,
And worketh willingly with her hands.
She is like the merchant-ships;
She bringeth her food from afar.
She riseth also while it is yet night,
And giveth meat to her household,
And their task to her maidens.
She considereth a field, and buyeth it:
With the fruit of her hands she planteth a vineyard.
She girdeth her loins with strength,
And maketh strong her arms.
She perceiveth that her merchandise is profitable:
Her lamp goeth not out by night.
She layeth her hands to the distaff,
And her hands hold the spindle.
She spreadeth out her hand to the poor;
Yea, she reacheth forth her hands to the needy.
She is not afraid of the snow for her household;
For all her household are clothed with scarlet.
She maketh for herself carpets of tapestry;
Her clothing is fine linen and purple.
Her husband is known in the gates,
When he sitteth among the elders of the land.
She maketh linen garments and selleth them;
And delivereth girdles unto the merchant.
Strength and dignity are her clothing;
And she laugheth at the time to come.

PROVERBS 31:10–25

A VIRTUOUS WOMAN

I.

She hasn't been dead four months and I've already eaten to the bottom of the deep freeze. I even ate the green peas. Used to I wouldn't turn my hand over for green peas.

My whole name is Blinking Jack Ernest Stokes, stokes the fire, stokes the stove, stokes the fiery furnace of hell! I've got a nerve problem in back of the face so I blink. June nicknamed me for it when she was little.

My wife's name was Ruby Pitt Woodrow Stokes. She was a real pretty woman. Used to I used to lay up in bed and say, "Don't take it off in the dark! I want to see it all!"

Ruby died with lung cancer in March. She wasn't but forty-five, young woman to die so early. She used to tell me, she'd say, "What's good for the goose is good for the gander. I imagine I'll stop smoking about the time you stop drinking." June's daddy, Burr, told me one time people feed on each other's bad habits, which might could be true except for one thing, I'm not really what I would call a drinking man. I hardly ever take a drink except when I need one.

But Ruby died and they laid her out and crossed her hands over her bosom, and I said to them, "I never saw her sleeping like that." They said but that's the way everybody was laid, so I said, "Fine then, I'll let her be."

I did lean over in the coffin though and fix her fingers so the nicotine stains wouldn't show. Ruby had the creamiest soft skin and I hated to have brown spots ruin her for people. Suppose you went to view somebody who'd died being shot or stabbed somewhere so you'd notice. Don't you know they'd fill in with some kind of spackle and smooth it over to match him? Sure they would! Same thing only different with Ruby's two ashy-smelling fingers.

God, you ought to've seen her in the hospital, weak, trying to sit up, limp as a dishrag. She'd lost down so much, looked like she'd literally almost shook all the meat off, all that coughing and spewing up she'd done. If you want to feel helpless as a baby sometime, you go somewhere and watch such as that. Seemed like every time she'd cough a cold shudder'd run up and down me.

I sat with her long as they'd let me that night, then I had to leave. I stuck my head up under her tent and said to her,

" 'Night 'night, Ruby. I'm headed back to the Ponderosa with Burr. I'll see you first thing in the morning." Then she put those two ashy-smelling fingers up to her mouth like either she was blowing me a kiss or telling me to hush a little. And while I was looking at her and trying to figure out which one she meant, I realized she wasn't motioning love or to hush to me. She was wanting a cigarette, asking me for one. I thought, Well I will be damned. And I said, Hard as that woman worked to get over too good a life then too bad a life, what a pity, what a shame to see this now.

I hated to but I had to call it selfish, not like the Ruby I knew. But I suppose when you're that bad off and you're not here, not gone either, I suppose you can get to the point that you are all that matters to yourself, and thinking about yourself is the last thing left you can remember how to do. So you're bound to go on and forgive it. And after it all, after it's all said and done, I'll still have to say, Bless you, Ruby. You were a fine partner, and I miss you.

2.

By Thanksgiving I'll have everything organized. I tie a package of pork with some corn, beef with some beans, and so forth, so all Jack should have to do is reach into the freezer and take out a good, easy meal. This should help him.

When I was out on the back porch working on that this morning I thought about how somebody, especially somebody who doesn't know us, would say, "That's the most morbid thing I've ever heard of." But there'd be others who'd say, "That Ruby sure is smart to make sure her husband's well-fed when she's gone." I don't know. I can't do much, but I can do something. There's not a whole lot a woman can do from the grave.

If we're careful this winter he'll have enough food to last three months, probably more. Then maybe he'll feel up to planning a garden, carrying the whole thing through by himself. But somehow, when I see him a year, two years from now, he's letting himself in Burr's house, hungry, lonesome, apologizing for interrupting supper for the third time that week, saying as long as he's there and there's a plenty he might ought to help him eat it. I don't know why I try to picture his life any other way, any independent way, when he's counted on me for so long. I know I'd give anything to be able to will what I wish to happen. Wouldn't any woman who loves her husband?

Another thing, I wish I could go back to the day I was diagnosed and change everything about it, not just the news, but the way Jack took the news and the way I handled him. He's so good to me, but when he said what he did that day I wanted to turn on him, against him. Sometimes we all could use a lesson in keeping quiet. Hard as it is, sometimes we need to hold back. He should've. I should've.

We came home from the doctor's office and I sat down with some coffee. He sat down with me, and I said, "What do you think's going to happen to me?" You know how you turn to somebody you love so they can help you. But all he said was, "Shoot woman! Not a damn thing! Anybody mean as the old squaw'll outlive everybody."

What'd he think? Did he expect me to laugh, slap my leg and say, "Ain't it the truth? I'm not dying. I'm not even sick!"

But I didn't. I cried. I cried and heaved and sobbed and wouldn't let him touch me. When he wanted to know what was going on I told him I didn't need his cheering up, that I was upset enough without him insulting me. He yelled at me, "Insulting?" And then he asked if I wanted him to call the undertaker and have him cart me off ahead of schedule or if I planned to just leave then and crawl out into the woods and wait for it to happen. I told him how far off the mark he was, how I wished he could get something right for once. Then I saw his face change, and I saw how badly I'd hurt him.

See, there's something raw and right there on the surface with him. Sometimes, I swear, he's just like a child. You have to be so careful. You can't ever just throw words out. They have to land somewhere, and they land on him and there he is so raw from the way he was raised, and then it's too late.

I kept to myself the rest of the day, kept all my thoughts to myself. And I hate to say it, but sometimes I just wanted to yank him and say, "Didn't you know cheering me up would do more harm than good? What possessed you to do the wrong thing when I needed the right thing the most? I don't ask for much from you. Can't you see that anything less than not exactly right hurts worse than I already hurt? You've got to cure me or either love me so strongly that I feel some of this pain pass from me. Those are the only things you have any business doing right now."

See, this is how Jack can be. I gave up a long time ago sending him to the store for something. You'd be better off sending a monkey. I'd ask him to walk down to Porter's store and pick up a few things and then I'd hand him the list and he'd step back like I was handing him a snake. He'd say, "I don't need a list." He wouldn't even look at it. He'd say, "Just tell it to me."

So I'd say, "Okay, a short loaf of white bread, margarine, cheese, and cornmeal," and nine times out of ten he'd walk back into this house with a long loaf of wheat bread, butter, cornmeal, but no cheese. And if I'd try to say anything, he'd harp on that cornmeal, going on and on about how he didn't mess up entirely. I'd try to say, "I know you got the cornmeal but I needed the other things too," and he'd hold his hand up like a teacher saying she's heard quite enough. You let that happen and your nerves will tell you not to send Blinking Jack Stokes out to the store anymore.

Sometimes when he'd come home missing an item or two he'd give me what he had and then he'd pull a little paper sack from his back pocket and say, "Sweets for my sweet." And there I'd be needing cheese or cornmeal or something to make supper, but I'd have a sack of candy. I couldn't fuss at him. All I could do was sit down at the table and take out a piece of the candy and suck on it mad and wonder about a man who runs out of cornmeal money buying peppermint for his wife. Candy couldn't help me then, can't help me now.

I think about Jack that day I was diagnosed and it all comes back clear as you please, my grandmother in the hospital. When she finally became too ill to be looked after at home my parents helped Big Daddy find a nursing hospital for her. She'd always lived right next door to us, and I got so lonesome for her that daddy let me spend weekends there with her.

Big Daddy'd always get there first thing Saturday morning. He'd pull a chair up by the bed and say, "How are you today, Sophie?" She'd never answer him. He'd take her arm and pat and rub it back and forth, back and forth, and then she'd jerk it away like he'd burned her. Then he'd realize he was rubbing the place where she'd had so many shots. But he'd take that arm and do the same thing every single visit, same thing, not thinking. Then he'd take his hat off and place it in his lap, reverently, like he was in church, not his church but some unfamiliar church he felt a little awkward in. She'd moan, trying to lift her head up to say something to him. Then he'd start talking, saying something about her nice begonias or her nice game hens or how nice her herb garden looked with the dew on it that morning or how fine a job Eloise was doing keeping everything just like she liked it. And then one time she got her head up off her pillow and she turned her full face to him and said in the hatefulest tone you can imagine, "Shut up! Go straight to hell! Leave me alone!"

Big Daddy looked like she'd shot him, and he turned around to me to see if I could help him, tell him how to react or jump in there for him. I didn't know what to do. She'd always been such a calm woman. But I'd know what to do now, and she knew what she needed then, but if you have to tell somebody then it doesn't count. It just doesn't. It's like sending yourself flowers on a birthday and signing the name of the man you love on the card.

If I could, I'd go back there and tell Big Daddy to lift her shoulders off of that bed and hold her and forget every last thing he'd always thought was best to say in times like these. See, he'd thought that bringing the things from home up close to her would make her feel better, as if she'd ever be back there, back on the beam. But she knew that those game hens scratching around in the yard were a whole life away from her. And he thought that by filling up that damp-smelling hospital room, and her mind, with all those things that we could all pretend everything would be fine, everything's going to be just fine. But she was dying! And it's not fair pretending. It's a bigger cheat than having to die.

If you want to see a man afraid just put him in a room with a sick woman who was once strong. See, I know now that this world is built up on strong women, built up and kept up by them too, them kneeling, stooping, pulling, bending, and rising up when they need to go and do what needs to get done. And when a man sees a woman like that sick and hurt, especially the kind of man who knows a woman's strength but can't confess it, when he sees her sick or hurt it terrifies him, like he's witnessing a chunk of the universe coming loose and he knows he doesn't have what it takes to stick it back together. And that man will feel guilty and foolish then too because he never made himself say what he always knew.

So a man, especially one like my grandfather, will see things coming apart and all he can do is rush to it, rush to it and hide the broken, chipped off, wrong piece. He'll slip it under something to pretend, or hope to pretend, it's not there, not one bit different from when a child hides a special toy he's broken.

That's all my grandfather was guilty of, fear, faith in his words, but that was a high crime in her eyes. That's all Jack was guilty of that day, but I've lived with him a good while and I believe I understand him. Sometimes it might take an afternoon or evening of being here in this kitchen alone, thinking, but I can usually come to see his reasons through his ways. And half the job of finding peace is finding understanding. Don't you believe it to be so?

3.

Ruby was the first and last woman I ever loved, outside of my mama, not meaning it to sound like she was one bit like mama though. Mama was a tough, hard woman, skin like cat tongue. You didn't run to be up next to her, if she'd have let you. It was her that'd say to come here, and she'd stand me between her knees and scrub the backs of my ears with a old rag and box lye soap, and she'd run a comb through my hair so hard I'd swear my head was bleeding. No, she wasn't the hugging kind of mama. I imagine it was all the Indian in her made her like she was.

I don't know how she and my daddy got up together. It wasn't something they sat around our house and went over. I have to see him proposing to her something like, "You need to marry me." And then he probably pulled her over up next to him and took her to a Holiness preacher for him to marry them. My daddy always was a Holiness man, always trying to shove Jesus down I and mama's throats. He drug me to church and tent revivals with him until I got too big to be beat into going. He'd start on mama on a Sunday morning and she'd walk outside and slam the door in his face talking, same thing every Sunday the sun rose.

She passed when I was fourteen, food poison. Turned out to be a bad piece of meat, but we thought first it was just the stomach flu. By the time daddy found out about the meat she was sick as a dog, just got sicker and sicker and couldn't anybody do a damn thing about it. There I was a boy and watching her and wanting to ask daddy, "Where's He now?"

It was something natural-born freakish about it, how the day she died it came the biggest snow we'd ever had, snow, then sleet, then snow on top of all of it. I remember carrying her out of the house and putting her in the wagon and the snow pure wanted to come up past I and daddy's knees. Then it was like pulling teeth making that mare drag that wagon with the wheels not hardly turning. Daddy had to borrow the money to bury her, borrowed about as much as we were worth.

After she was gone I missed her, hard as she was, I did miss her. I'd close my eyes in the bed at night and think about her, about her being part Cherokee, high cheekbones, and I'd see her dressed like one, feathers, and she'd be walking across a hot bed of coals, not flinching a bit, just like she used not to flinch when she'd scald a chicken, dip it in the cast-iron pot outside and it steaming, and pluck it faster than you could yell, "You better let it cool!" But she didn't mean to let it cool. She'd pluck it and it'd be ready to go. But not Ruby. No, that wasn't Ruby. She never even liked the dishwater over a certain degree and she always kept her a tube of lotion up on the windowsill over the sink.

I'd always have to think of my mama whenever Ruby made a pie, which was every Sunday morning until she got so weak she couldn't hardly crawl out of the bed. She'd always hold that pie up on one hand and turn it round and round very slow and put a crimp in the crust with a butter knife. Mama would've been put off by Ruby's pies, too much, too good. She wouldn't have said a word though if she'd walked in on Ruby crimping one. She'd have just gazed at that pie and walked out. Sometimes now, even with me being as old a man as I am, sometimes I want to ask mama why she couldn't ever have made I and daddy just one pie, just a plain one. But I just guess a hard woman like my mama didn't think about dessert. That's all okay now. I lived a long time with a soft woman and her soft way of doing things. I excuse the pies I didn't have because I was satisfied by Ruby's so many times.

I know people generally think if you act like Ruby, do

like she used to and all, I know they think you bound to've had it easy all along, not like mama, not like a man either that walks around with his fists up all the time because he knows he'd better. But think that about Ruby and be dead wrong.

Burr's ex-wife, Tiny Fran, despised Ruby for carrying herself like she was somebody, and I said to Burr one time, I said, "You know, it shows a bad weakness in a woman when all she can do is find fault, be ridiculing." And all he was able to do was say, "I know it. Tiny Fran's hard on everybody but herself and Roland." Roland's her old jailbird boy.

But see, the thing about Ruby is, her mama and daddy might've been able to give her a nice, easy road to go down when she was little, but the minute she could she lit out of there and hit a skid, big skid named John Woodrow. Now I just have to shake my head at how it didn't kill her, that taking that wide turn off that easy road.

He's the one that showed her how to smoke, damn his soul. Sometimes I've wished I'd been the one to kill him. Lord God, I think of them married together and I see that little shack he had her in, and then I see buzzards flying round and round the chimney, waiting to swoop down and take what'd be left of them when the way they were living finished with them. And then I see me, the biggest buzzard of them all, circling too, circling Ruby, waiting.

I think about it and think how it's odd how it all lined up for me, all that grief and misery lining up into something so good. There her husband was about dead, then dead, and there I was, ready, willing, more than willing to hop in his spot and have her for my own. Everybody encouraged me. They all said, "You ought not to let that girl slip away out from under you, not with you a good man and needing a wife." Everybody, Burr, everybody at the store, they all said how if I played my cards right I might could have her. And I did, and I never regretted it, not even now with her powder smell and her cooking smell and the way she could talk to me, not even with all that gone, gone buried with her in the grave. All I hate is being back to being by myself.

Ruby got left out here by herself, mama and daddy on the other end of the state and she too ashamed to go back home. I told her long as she was here she might as well stay, and she did. All the whole time I was hoping it wasn't showing through how I meant not just to stay but to stay with me, marry me.

To tell the truth, I'd have to say I thought I'd bust before I got to her house that night to tell her that old sorry John Woodrow was dead. See, I'd been the one to tell her he'd been hurt, cut, and I said to myself, Carrying her the news of him dying, being there with a shoulder and so forth, this'll be good, timely, this ought to get me in good.

Think what you will! Shock, shock! I don't give a damn. If I gave a damn I would've kept it to myself. I had to do what I had to do. See, a man like me does what he needs to do more often than he wants to, and I saw Ruby and I had to have her, needed her. She was the most gorgeous thing I'd ever seen in my life, sitting under Lonnie Hoover's big pecan tree that morning like a prize, and the thought of me going long as I had without one made me think, started me to think that I might could try for this girl. You get to be forty out here and you think about things like chances and prizes passed by, dried up, you drying up and passing without somebody to love and love you back.

She wasn't but twenty then, and me forty, and it was almost five months from the day I met her that I married her. I know what it sounds like, like a old lecher got him a child-bride when her first husband wasn't even cold yet. Go ahead and think it. It just shows how much you don't know me, or Ruby.

But Lord, did she evermore have one sorry time with John Woodrow. It embarrassed her to tell me all how she lived, like I'd judge her for it and think less of her. No, Ruby! I loved you more!

He made her live in one falling-down place right after the other, migrant houses, trailers, places he scrounged up for them to rent. And half the time he wouldn't work. They'd have to depend on what she could go out and do and bring in. That's sorriness. A woman, especially one built small like Ruby, has about as much business picking cucumbers as a child does. I told her when we got married, I said, "If you want to get a job working, then for God's sakes let's find you something to do in the cool inside." But she just wanted to stay here and run the house. Ruby loved to run a house. It took her a while to get in the track, but I didn't care. I liked just watching her moving around the kitchen.

But on back. Ruby said one day she came in from the field and found John Woodrow laid up with some old young greasy gal and there was a baby greasy as his mama crawling around on the floor. I asked her what she did and she said she took and left and went and bought a pistol from a man and came back aiming to shoot him. I thought, Lord God! I featured Ruby going up to somebody buying a pistol and it scared me to death.

But she never got the chance to shoot him. I've got the pistol now. I use it to blow cans off the top of the trash barrel. A few years ago I joined the NRA. People don't want to believe I've got my card but I've got one. Ruby took and had plastic put on it because she said I was going to wear it out taking it out of my wallet so much.

Seems like I'm always having to take something out and show somebody the truth about something they don't want to believe. I guess if you have on a new suit or drive a new car or live in town you might could get somebody to believe you. But Ruby always said that my talking loud wouldn't make people listen to me any better than if I talked regular. She said people will usually decide by looking at you if they think what you have to say's worth a hoot. And she told me you can't change that because you can't change people and that's that and you have to just go on and do the best you can with it. I think that's a damn shame in this world.

4.

I've never told Jack this. I wouldn't spoil his time for anything in the world, but every single time I hear that gun go off all I can think of is John Woodrow. I know if Jack had any idea that was happening, especially now with me sick, I know he'd sell the gun or even give it away. I can see him out the kitchen window, just on the edge of the pines, taking aim. He couldn't hit the broad side of a barn, but that's never seemed to bother him.

He really latched onto that pistol. At first, I didn't think anything of it, but lately when he goes out there, it's all I can do to keep from running out and grabbing it and pitching it into the woods and daring him to go in and find it. Then I get upset and he comes back in, looks at me and says, "What's the matter with you, Ruby?" And what do I say? I say, "I just missed you, that's all." Well, it may not be the whole truth, but it gets us by. Then he'll kiss me. He doesn't make light of tears anymore.

But talk about truth, what truth did I ever have with John Woodrow? None. I don't believe he ever spoke a word of truth to me, except maybe when he thought a dash of the truth might get him what he wanted.

Why'd I marry him? I think part of the reason is that I didn't have enough sense to say no, plain and simple. I'm not saying I was ignorant. I knew the difference between right and wrong, but it was a vague sort of knowing, and it didn't occur to me that what I was doing that second, the second it took to tell John Woodrow I'd marry him, was terribly wrong, the kind of wrong that can ruin your life. Deep down though, I must have suspected something wasn't quite right, or why would I have waited until my father and brothers were working in the farthest field before I packed my bags?

I'd rehearsed the question all through my childhood, and I'd dreamed of it coming but I just didn't know when I could expect it. All I knew for sure was that somehow I became available at sixteen. And I said, One day a man's going to come along and say the kindest things to me and buy me things and then he'll say something on the order of "Come live with me and be my love." I had the two of us on my long porch, moon shining through the trees and so forth.

And who was the first one to come along and pay me a bit of attention but John Woodrow? I was eighteen, just graduated from high school. I'd planned to enter a Presbyterian college the next fall and study piano. It was about the only thing I knew how to do. But John Woodrow was twenty-six, and not a thing going for him but his looks. I might could say he had brains working for him, but he put his smarts to such a bad use that I wouldn't feel right calling him intelligent. He's the only person I've ever known, except maybe Roland Stanley, who'd lie when telling the truth would do him more good. Now can you call that smart? And what about me? He lied to me and I ate up every word that came out of his mouth. Oh, he was a hoodlum through and through, and there I was, lonesome, bored to tears, and there was my family, my mama and daddy and two big brothers, loving me like I was a big baby doll.

I remember how hard I watched him all the first week he worked. I'd cut through the yard when he was out there just to see him better, so he could see me. Then my girl-friend and I saw him with a couple of the other workers in town, in the movie lobby. And I remember pointing him out to Jean Anne and she said, "He looks just like Tab Hunter! Just clean him up a little, put some pleated pants on him, and he's just the spitting image." I think that right that minute I shaped his hair, cleaned his fingernails, took a tuck in his pants here and there and got an idea of him that stayed with me until after we were married, when the bad times started. I've heard that you can want to see something so badly that you can convince yourself to really see it, and I know it to be true. I even convinced my-self that his idea of courtship, which was sending word up to the house through one of the women in the crew to meet him in town at such-and-such a time and place, I even started to believe that was romantic. I said, This'll eventu-ally be another Peyton Place, me against my family, me in the right and them not understanding my feelings and so forth. But it was never any me against mama and daddy. Either one of them would've gladly died for the baby girl, and look what I was doing to them. Even after everything happened and I finally went home, tail between my legs, after all that time I'd stayed gone, mama and daddy just wanted to know if I was okay, if I had any money in my pocket, if John Woodrow had hurt me. They said they would've gone out after me but they knew I'd be back in my own time, which I did after I married Jack and felt like I could face them.

Looking back on it all, I think the mistake I made with John Woodrow had more to do with the careful way they raised me than anything else. Growing up, I had abso-lutely no idea anything bad could happen in a life because nothing bad had happened in mine, no catastrophes. My grandmother died but mama and daddy helped me through it, and I'd spent so much time with her, watching her get weaker and weaker, that I felt like dying was the next step for her, something that naturally should happen next.

But worse than my ignorance of any bad coming into a life was the fact that I didn't have the imagination, the pure imagination to see that hard things or ugly things might happen farther on down the road. I was just whistling along. I can't remember making decisions on my own. I might've made a mistake, and that was something my parents were real careful about. It took me a long time to learn that mistakes aren't good or bad, they're just mistakes, and you clean them up and go on. In my case, I buried my mistake and got married again, and just trusted my insides to tell me I hadn't made another one. But anyway, my parents protected me from bad choices by making the choices for me. And alot of it had to do with me being the baby girl in the family. My mama was the kind of woman who believed girls in girl clothes are less apt to get in trouble than girls dressed like boys. I remember begging her for some pants to play outside in, and when she finally made me some she sewed eyelet around the cuffs, just a touch of girl on those pants. And my daddy and brothers were just as bad. If I had a tough piece of meat on my plate, the minute one of them saw me struggling they'd lean over, take my knife and fork from me and cut the meat up for me. I never rebelled against it, snatched my knife back and said, "I'll cut my own meat up, thank you." All the women in my family were calm women. They wouldn't have said a word. It was just the way things were. The only woman I knew who wasn't calm was Sudie Bee, our housekeeper. She ran the house for mama, and how could she do all she did and not get ruffled, not make some decisions and some mistakes? I just hated that the first big decision I ever made was the kind that can kill you if you make a mistake, and it almost killed me.

When John Woodrow asked me to marry him I might as well have been in a school play, hearing what I thought was my cue and asking the teacher, "Is this when I say my part?" And she says to go ahead so I say, "Yes, yes I will." Then everybody's supposed to clap and nod and sing your praises, and then they throw rice at you on your way out, and you take all your pretty presents and put them in his car and drive off. But that's not the way it turned out, play, marriage, nothing.

I can see mama on the front steps, yelling that she's going to go find my daddy and brothers and tell them to come stop me. But I tell her I've already decided I'm leaving with him, and I roll up the car window so I don't have to hear her. I can see her though. John Woodrow drives this old car he's borrowed all up on the lawn turning around, and we leave mama there crying.

I was crying too, but I thought time would take care of me, that once we had our rings and a nice honeymoon hotel that everything would be just fine. I'd call daddy and we'd chat just like Elizabeth Taylor and Spencer Tracy in *Father of the Bride*, one of those daydreamy movies that had contributed to the mess I was in. But that didn't happen. I got no ring, no nice honeymoon hotel, just a quickie thrown together mess and humiliation. As soon as I left my mama I knew something was wrong, but I didn't know how I'd gotten myself into this, and I surely didn't know how to get myself out. That sort of thing comes from one too many suppers of having someone reach over to cut your meat for you.

If I'd had the good sense to turn John Woodrow down I could've waited for somebody else to come along, and I bet he would've been a nice boy, probably somebody I'd known all my life. And we would've gotten married with both our families there, and we'd have built a house on a piece of land daddy'd have given us, and that'd be that. A hail storm every few years or maybe a miscarriage would've been the only troubles we'd have seen.

That's how my parents were. They sat down at the dining room table and made out Christmas cards together, and I licked the stamps. They took my brothers and me to the capital every September to buy school clothes, and we always spent the night there and went to a movie or a play.

Sudie Bee and her husband, Lester, lived in an apartment off the side of our house and we were taught to respect them as much as we did each other. We never ran or yelled in the house, and we always used cloth napkins, company or no company.

And mama and daddy were both good-looking people, mama especially. She was just vain enough to be funny about it. Every time before they went out to dinner she'd check herself in the long mirror, turning around and smoothing her dress down over her hips, asking him if she looked all right. He'd say, "Pretty as a picture. I'll be beating men back with a stick."

I remember having to stay at home those nights with Sudie Bee, and I'd imagine mama and daddy out together, everybody looking at mama, admiring her. I'm sure they did. Nobody would've looked at them and said, "Look at that country-come-to-town over there." Daddy was the kind of man who couldn't finish a meal somewhere without at least one person coming over to the table, shaking his hand and introducing his wife or his son or somebody. People knew he ran a good farm, a big place, and they respected him for it. He served two terms, maybe more, as a county commissioner, and I can barely remember holding the scissors with mama, helping her cut his picture out of the paper when he won a Ruritan award.

You don't find it much better than that. My parents did

a fine job raising us, the kind of job that most people say they plan to do but just don't have it in them to ever get done. But they sure had it, all the love and strength day in and day out. And even though they never taught me to handle the kinds of decisions I'd need to make about John Woodrow, they did teach me self-respect, and self-respect should've protected me from John Woodrow's advances.

I should've said, Ruby, you love yourself and your home too much to insult either one with this excuse of a man, but I didn't. Oh but I had enough self-respect to pack my nicest underwear and my pretty gown and robe set, and I thought enough of myself to make sure I was clean and powdery for the trip from home. And I also had enough self-respect left to cry when he ripped my robe and my gown and pawed at my nice underwear. And there was enough left to tell him not to do that anymore, that he'd hurt me. But I more than made up for that in ignorance and dreaming, believing him when he said he was sorry and believing every other lie he told me.

See, he had me convinced he came from something, that the only reason he was working migrant labor was because his brother and sister had ruined him. He said they made sure he didn't get his cut of their daddy's farm, talked him down to their father and so forth, made up a pack of lies and got themselves good and set up. And when their father died, poor John Woodrow was left out in the cold.

He was a real victim, which then, to me, was the exact same thing as a real hero, only different, as Jack would say. He said he was trying to work his way back up from the bottom, but so far the only good to come from his efforts was me, that if he hadn't been working on daddy's farm that summer we would never have met. Don't you know it to be so!

See, daddy had added extra acreage that spring and our usual help wasn't nearly enough to manage the crop, so he had to do something he didn't want to do, hire migrant labor. They stayed in a camp a few miles from our house, and every morning at dawn an old rusty truck would pull up under the big sycamore tree and what looked to me like a hundred men and women would crawl out of it and go spread out on the grass and sleep until daddy and Lester took them to the fields. And I can remember standing at the kitchen window with mama, and she'd look out at them and comment on how dusty and dirty they all looked for it to be so early in the day. I don't think she ever accepted the fact that not everybody in the world takes, or even wants, a nice hot tub bath before bed. And I know this now as well as I know myself, if my daddy had known I'd take up with one of those men sleeping in that yard he'd have let the crops burn in the fields before he'd have let a migrant worker on his land.

I can also remember the first day they worked and how

Sudie Bee told mama she'd better send to the store for some picnic plates to feed them on. She said they would break mama's good things, and to be safe, we'd better fix a buffet on a table outside and let them eat in the yard. Mama said that wouldn't be necessary, that she had more than enough serving pieces and so forth, and that there was plenty of room around the long table on the side porch.

Sudie Bee just said, "Go ahead and get your family's dishplates busted up. See if Sudie Bee cares." I listened to both sides, and I had to agree with mama. These people would be tired, hot, hungry, and they'd appreciate a cool porch and a square meal. And all the time I was helping Sudie Bee get the dishes down she was mumbling things like, "She be coming up saying she 'gwine listen to old Sudie Bee next time, all them dishplates busted up."

We set a good table for them and then the three of us started our lunch in the kitchen. When mama heard them coming up in the yard she went to the side door and yelled out for them to come on in, that there was more than a plenty and they should just come on in and eat, make themselves right at home. Sudie Bee said, "She 'gwine find out. Be like telling the pig family make they-selves at home." But they came on in, and when we heard water running in the utility sink, mama looked at Sudie Bee and said, "See? They're washing up." Sudie Bee said that's what it sounded like and that Lester'd be in that utility room all night mopping up the flood and fixing the stopped up drain pipe. Mama didn't say anything back, but I knew she was thinking Sudie Bee had too little faith in her fellow man. I knew she was because I was thinking that myself, and I was my mama's girl.

When they left we went out there and Sudie Bee just stood at the end of the porch and said, "You be listening to me next time." Plates on the floor, under the table, in the chairs, food everywhere, butter turned out in the tea pitcher, not to mention the mess in the utility room, towels crammed in the toilet and so forth. Sudie Bee started scraping and stacking dirty plates, motioning up and down the window ledges with a fork at how most of the leaves had been stripped off the ferns. And the only time I can ever remember hearing my mama swear was when she saw how they'd used her African violet for an ashtray. She used to water the roots of that plant with a syringe.

The next day Sudie Bee made big platters of sandwiches and potato chips and I helped her put everything out on the picnic table. But you can bet mama didn't help. She stayed in her bedroom reading most of the morning. She'd been stung and she knew it, and she didn't want to be up close to those people until she knew she was ready, and a person like my mama is never ready.

We saw what people who don't care can do to people who do care about things, even if those things are only glasses and plates. What the things are, what they're worth in dollars, all that just isn't the point. But instead of running away from it, like mama did, I rushed to it and tried to forgive and understand it. That's all very well and good. That's a perfectly fine way to be, but not if one of those men out there urinating all over your mama's rose bushes has his eye on you.

That eating outside business was one of the things John Woodrow started throwing up in my face when we'd been married not more than a week or two. He said it showed how my family was too uppity, too picky, and way, way too rich. And nothing I could've ever told him would've changed his mind about us. But like a fool, I kept trying. I should've known he was lying about his own past as soon as he started ridiculing mine. But sometimes the hardest things in the world to see are the ones that are right up on you.

It never occurred to him that my daddy might've simply worked for what we had, that we weren't rich by any means, that we just looked that way from where he was situated. My parents might've taken us to the city to buy school clothes and all, but I know for a fact that the trip was planned three months ahead of time and budgeted down to the penny. But all John Woodrow could see was us riding off on a wild spree, throwing money out of the car windows, daddy draping furs all over mama in some fancy store while my brothers and I gorged ourselves on big milkshakes. Hearing him talk like that used to drive me crazy. I'd get so frustrated!

And once I had been away from home a while, he figured I'd chime in with him when he was being so cruel about my family. He'd try and shame me into saying something ugly so I could lower myself, so he could lord that over me. And when I didn't he found fault with everything I did. I remember the first time he called me a bitch. The only times I'd ever heard the word were on a schoolbus, mean boys running down the teacher. Hearing him yell that at me made me almost sick to my stomach. Like most everything he was saying to me by then, it made me cry, and that got him even hotter with me. Know why he called me that? Because I said just because we were married didn't mean he could do anything to me or with me that he pleased. No, I wasn't a bitch. I was just a good country girl who'd married this man and bitten off way, way more than she could chew.

Somebody could say, "If she loved her family so much, why didn't she run away and call someone to come get her?" I thought about it a hundred times a day, believe you me. Sometimes that was all I had to think about except how my body hurt. What would I have said? "Daddy, did you ever hear of *Tobacco Road*? Well, the situation I'm in is alot like that, only we're moving from place to place and I'm never sure where I am. So next summer when the migrants sit under our sycamore tree, don't think of anyone else but me. Okay, daddy?" And the funny thing about all this is how one of my big ambitions had always been to travel, not just to the state parks and such my parents had taken us to, but to exciting places around the country, maybe some foreign places. I'll tell you what, I travelled all right. Join a migrant crew, see the world! And I did. It was all foreign to me then, raggedy people, raggedy houses, children waiting at the ends of bean rows, scratching ringworms. I guess before I left with him I thought that wherever we pulled up to work a Sudie Bee would walk out under a cool tree and spread out ham sandwiches. That was a joke. I'd have come nearer thriving on John Woodrow's love than the food we had.

I started to get an edge on me though, something I'd never had. Oh, I'd had such a funny idea about what it took to be a woman. Little did I know back when I stayed propped up by the kitchen counter watching Sudie Bee cut up a chicken or roll out dough that I'd become a woman heating up yesterday's corned beef hash in a little tin house stuck in the middle of the kind of place my mama never liked to drive through.

Towards the end of the first winter with him he got on a wild loop about putting some money together and moving us to a town somewhere, being a family and so forth. He'd talk about it all night long, and when I finally asked him how he intended to raise the money, since it took everything we made to live, he said I was going to call daddy and ask him for my third of the inheritance early.

I told him that was the craziest thing I'd ever heard, but that wasn't what he wanted to hear from me, not after he'd spent all winter spending daddy's money in that twisted up head of his. I told him what he should do is call his own family, that they might be ready to make up for the trouble they'd caused him, that they might be feeling bad about what they'd done. It made sense to me. I was ready to get out of that mess we were living in myself, and I thought I was just helping him find another way to get that done.

You should've seen how he blew up at me, saying how stupid I was and so forth. And then one thing led to another and I found out all I needed to know about John Woodrow and his lies and traps and how much trouble a girl can get into believing in the movies.

This was his situation. About the only truth he'd told me about his family was that they hated him as much as he hated them. That's where the truth started and stopped both. And when he let it all out, he said he'd gone after his daddy with a butcher knife and missed, but he left and came back that night and burned every tobacco barn on the place to the ground. And it also came out that the farm was hardly big enough to support them, hardly anything worth dividing among three children. He said he was sent up three years for arson and when he got out his family wouldn't claim him, even had him put under a peace bond, which he broke when he stole his sister's car and ran it up a telephone pole. That's how he got the long scar by his knee, not in the high school football game he'd described to me the first night we slept together, which makes my skin crawl to even think about now.

About then is when I started smoking. He'd ridiculed me for not having any vices to speak of ever since we were married. He'd say, "I bet little Miss Vanderbilt don't even take liquor in her mint julep." I'd never even seen a mint julep, but I know he was picturing me sipping one on our long porch, long crinolined dress, Sudie Bee fanning and fetching for me, Lester down at the other end shining Paul and Jimmy's shoes. That's how his mind worked.

But see, before we were married no vices were more of a virtue, or so he made it seem. I think now I lit up that first cigarette because I was sick of listening to him, and I smoked the second one because I liked the way I felt after the first one. And all through that winter and on up until two months ago I smoked like a fiend. The reasons for doing it left but that never mattered. It's funny how something I used so long ago to get me by, a way I had of coping with things, it's just funny how it stayed with me to hurt me. And I let it, and ashamed as I am to say it, I'd die for a cigarette right now, but that's being taken care of. This would hurt my mama.

But the rest of that winter with him and on into the spring I'd talk myself into calling home and then talk myself right back out of it, smoking one cigarette right after the other, chewing my fingernails to the quick. Then the hotter it got, the iller he seemed to get at me. I remember how grateful I felt when he started staying in town all night. Whenever we got to a new place he could sniff out a pool hall and be headed there before I was in the door good. And there I'd be, left over from this big mess of a dream I'd put together without seeing that there wasn't any way it was going to turn out, and I was left there in it, with it.

Going to the Hoovers' farm turned out to be the salvation although it sure didn't look that way from the car window, all those tobacco fields hot and thick, and I said to myself driving by, If I have to work another day in this nasty, sticky heat I will surely die. I'd never seen it so hot.

Then no sooner than we got unpacked John Woodrow took off without a word. He stayed gone all night, and when he didn't show up the next morning the crew chief said that made the third time and he was fired. And I thought, Well Ruby, you asked for it. Then he told me I was going to help in the house, and I should stay around in the yard and wait for the Hoover women to wake up and come get me. I know he was thinking I'd look better at the big house than any of the others, and he probably also thought I looked like I didn't have the gall to steal anything. That's a high recommendation.

Frances Hoover called me inside a little later and told me she wanted this and that clean, and she said, "When I say clean I mean clean." She said her daughter was getting married there that next week and she expected everything to be done just right. I started in the kitchen, and while I was mopping the pantry I heard her yell up the stairs, "Tiny Fran, you get your majesty's self down here and help with this cleaning. I mean it, I'm not telling you again!" And then I heard somebody yell from the top of the stairs, "I already told you I'm sick!" Then Frances started again, "You get down here!" And they went back and forth yelling at each other until Frances popped her dust cloth on the banister and stomped up the stairs. The next thing I heard was skin being slapped. Tiny Fran came downstairs, the stairs were in the kitchen, and I could see she wasn't the one who'd been slapped. She looked real pleased with herself, and all I could think was, My God! That girl just hit her mama! Then she went to the refrigerator and poured herself a big glass of chocolate milk, saw me standing by the pantry and said to me, "Hand me a box of soda crackers in there. I feel like shit this morning. And who the hell are you?" I told her my name and that I was there to help her mama. When I got her the crackers she snatched them from me and said, "Well good, that woman needs all the help she can get." I was just amazed. I didn't know what I'd walked in on, that topsy-turvy house.

What a time I was to have with Tiny Fran! Everything she touched seemed to come out wrong, be it her fault or not, nothing worked out. But ever since we met that day at least she's had somebody to blame. She lives in town now. I haven't seen her in a long time, but I wouldn't be half surprised to hear that when she drops an egg or burns the butter she screams out, "Damn you, Ruby Stokes!" I wouldn't be surprised at all. She never came very far from where she was the day we met, mad at the whole world, settling her stomach with soda crackers and undoing all the good that was doing with a quart of chocolate milk, then sick again and frustrated and not understanding why.

5.

I'd be lying if I didn't say how the reason I had to wait so long to get married is nobody would have me. And it's not like I gave a crowd of women the opportunity to turn me down. I never asked a one. I never came close to asking. Until I met Ruby I suppose the sweetest thing I'd ever asked a woman to do for me was to hold a mule still while I hitched the plow to him.

I had the big mouth with Ruby though, going all into how I'd been waiting for the right one to come along, saving myself and so forth. She could've looked right in my face and said, "Bullshit. You were born a dried up skinny man and here you are expecting me to think you let a world of women pass you by, more plowboy than playboy." But she didn't laugh at me. All she said was she wanted somebody to take care of her, and if I promised to, she'd marry me. I said then, I say now, "That's the best thing in the world for me, for the both of us, best thing for anybody to do for somebody." You hear tell of somebody saying how so-and-so made him feel like a real man, how so-and-so made somebody feel like a natural woman and so forth, it's all the time on the television and the radio, you hear all about that and I can honestly say that before I married Ruby I'd felt like a boy on the outside looking in, but Ruby, when she loved me, I said, This is what it must feel like to be a man. Before then if somebody'd walked up to me and asked me right out who I was I'd have said, "A tenant, one of the boys the Hoovers use," but now I'd say, "I'm the man that was married to Ruby."

I was hauling manure to the garden the day I came across her sitting under the tree, and I thought how perfect a picture she'd make if she had a flower or some sewing, something womany in her hand besides a cigarette. So I went right up to her, running on pure gall or what must've already been love, and I spoke to her on her smoking. You'd think that with somebody, a stranger like her all of a sudden there one morning in the yard I'd been hauling manure across all my life, you'd think I'd be too bound up to breathe, much less speak. But I didn't bind up. I leaped right in. I didn't bind up hardly at all.

And when she talked to me it was none of this twisting and twirling of the hair and this and that kind of eye-batting. No, I'd ask her a question and she'd answer it. She'd ask me one and I'd answer it back. See, that's a time being skinny and not good-looking will do you some good. If I'd been real smooth it might've triggered her to act like a woman will around somebody real smooth, twirling the hair and what-not. But me being like I was, am, let me get a foot in the door. So she just talked to me like she knew I didn't mean her harm, not out there in the yard, not ever. I thought talking to her, I thought, This is the kind of woman I could get along with. Ruby, you're my kind of woman!

But while we were talking there, I started looking at her hard and I said to myself, This woman, look at her skin, she's not one of these that pull up with the migrant crews. It was like the feeling you get when you see a car with out-of-state tags pull up at the store, and somebody gets out and everybody in there has to stop and examine them. So I looked at her good and listened to her, listened to her lie to me, and thought how she was the kind of woman, girl really, that some tough somebody'd love to chew up and spit out. After she told me how she was married and had a husband and his name was John Woodrow and all, I said, Well, I ought to tell her what I heard, I ought to. So I did. It liked to've shocked her. Then I said, Well, you told her, the least thing you can do is offer to help her out. So I told her where all I lived and to come on if she needed something.

She acted like she would. Then about that time I heard Tiny Fran stick her head out and yell at her, "Come on in here and find where you laid the soda crackers yesterday. I'm sick as a dog this morning." I thought to myself, Just like Tiny Fran to be yelling her old sorry business out the back door. And I said, I sure hope it doesn't take this girl long to get Tiny Fran's number. You always needed her number to handle her, to try to anyway. I didn't know back then that handling Tiny Fran was something Ruby'd have to do more often than she'd have liked to. But now I think I can look back to that first day with Ruby and feel like it was the whole start of many more things than that. Sometimes I feel like everything started with Ruby.

6.

I got things sufficiently clean for Frances. All day she kept after Tiny Fran to help me but she kept telling her mama things like scrubbing floors wasn't in her job description. I worked around her most of the day. Sometimes it seemed like she intentionally put herself in my way so I'd have to say, "Excuse me." I thought she might be pregnant but I wasn't sure, not then. She was already a large girl so it was difficult to tell exactly.

But I worked all day there and went home after Frances ran her inspection and said I should come back the next day and do the upstairs. So I went on and when I got to that little place we were staying in, I still can't believe this, but when I got there I saw something that stopped me absolutely stone still.

John Woodrow was there, yes he was surely back, just

lying there on the cot, lying there propped up on a pillow, smoking a cigarette, and some girl not more than sixteen was prancing up and down in front of him, wearing my nice underwear, modeling for him, wearing those things I'd carried around with me all that time wrapped up in the tissue paper they'd come in, the nice things he'd tried to tear off me on our honeymoon. I'd washed those things and folded them back up and packed them away at the bottom of my bag where I didn't think he'd find them and ruin them. And there she was with them on. And that's not the half of it. She had a little baby crawling around on the floor, trying to keep up with her, with a diaper on I could smell from the door. I felt sick to my stomach. He saw me and she saw me and they were both so drunk, or in his case so sorry and so drunk, that they didn't even rush to cover up. He called out, "Ruby!" But not like he'd been caught, like he wanted me to come on in and join his party. I'd never been so disgusted in my life. I slammed the door and ran out and sat down on the edge of the wheat field. I remember how the wheat felt good to me, sad and angry as I was. And I sat there and said, What am I going to do about this? I wanted to kill him. To tell the truth, that's exactly what I wanted to do. But I knew I couldn't. I couldn't have lived with myself if I'd taken a life, even a life as worthless as John Woodrow's. But I said, You can hurt him. You don't have to kill him but you can surely make him miserable. Migrant people got cut, shot all the time, well, not all the time, but certainly enough for me to think if I shot John Woodrow in the leg or something that I'd not be called to answer for it the way I would be if we weren't on the migrant circuit. And I thought if I played my cards right, provoked a fight with him, let some other people along that long row of shacks hear it, I thought if I pushed him far enough he'd explode and try to hurt me and I'd defend myself. Then I'd have no choice but to pack up and go back home. So I bought a pistol from a man and went back to that little shack bound and determined to do some damage to old John Woodrow. And I wasn't afraid as you'd think I'd be, having only been around guns when I used to go skeet shooting with my brothers. I was only afraid he'd get it away from me before I could use it and that'd be all she wrote.

When I got back to the house John Woodrow and his girlfriend had cleared out, cleared out and took my lingerie with them. But I said, That's all right. I'll wait. And I waited and waited, fell asleep that night with my clothes on, waiting for him to come in, but little did I know I'd seen the last of him.

I went back to the Hoovers' when I woke up that next morning, and I left the pistol hidden under my pillow. I didn't take it with me because having a pistol in a migrant house is one thing, having it on you in the Hoovers' home would be another. See, one was society, the other wasn't. The rules are different, or, there're rules in one place and none in the other.

Frances had me clean everything but the light bulbs that day. I'd never had any experience cleaning a bathroom or a kitchen or even dusting a dresser, but you don't have to know how to clean to clean. I learned that real fast. If you know what clean looks like then you just take a mop or a broom or a rag and go at whatever's dirty until it's clean. That's that. And I knew clean. Sudie Bee could fly through a house, picking up things with one hand and cleaning under them with the other. She and Lester could roll up a rug, hang it outside, beat it, and lay it back down faster than alot of people could vacuum one. She scrubbed our shower doors like they were something alive that had to be beaten back. Yes, I surely knew the meaning of clean.

When Lonnie came in for lunch I overheard her telling him all the things she'd had me do, like taking everything out of the linen closet and wiping the shelves down. When he told her he doubted if anybody coming to the wedding would run a white glove in there, she said, "I know, but it seems like such a shame to waste good seasonal help." Then she told him she wanted to have me keep working in the house, cleaning, keeping things in order, and then she told him she also wanted me to serve and pick up at Tiny Fran's reception. He said, "I thought you already asked one of the girls from the Butler place," and she said, "I know

I did, but I like the idea of having this girl better." All old Frances wanted to do was show off white help, a white girl walking around her living room carrying a tray. And all I could think was how that'd be a new low in the life of Ruby Pitt Woodrow. Sudie Bee would never have put on a black dress and a little white apron and offered little sandwiches to people, but then again, nobody ever asked her to. She'd have brought her nephew Whistle Dick to serve and keep empty cups and plates picked up, not much different from what I did at Tiny Fran's wedding. I remembered mama and daddy's anniversary party, how Sudie Bee peeked out of the kitchen door and caught Whistle Dick tasting something off the buffet. He came back in the kitchen and Sudie Bee told him, "Your mama say you ain't got good sense, so I let you work for me doing something don't take sense, and Mr. Pitt he pay you good money, and then you be sticking your old fingers in somebody's food. You aint got to be no nigger just 'cause you black. And ain't nobody in there 'gwine ask you to wipe they nose. You just picking up plates! You mess up and then what Sister 'gwine do fo' money?" And all the time I was working at the reception, especially after I heard another one of Frances's remarks, it was all I could do to keep my fingers off the wedding cake, and the more I thought of Whistle Dick, the more I wanted to. Then I'd have been out, just like he was when Sudie Bee caught him sneaking the pineapple slices off a ham.

7.

Ruby got here the week before Burr got married, married to damn old Tiny Fran and her already starting to poke out some with Roland, lounging around all day, swinging in the porch swing and pulling out the front of her dress and blowing down it, yelling up to her mama's bedroom window about how hot she was. Her mama used to tell her to go somewhere and cool off. She'd tell her, "I can't change the temperature. Big people get hotter faster, you know that." And that'd piss Tiny Fran off, plump plus being pregnant. She'd hop up out of that swing and go inside, slamming doors, cussing like a sailor, saying how she was going to show her mama the back of her hand and so forth. She would too! And I'd think, Yeah, and either one of you let Lonnie know what all goes on and he'll take and use one of you to beat the other one with. If I'd been her daddy I'd have had to slap that sorriness back away from my supper table and said, "Get on away from here, you road whore!" I don't have the patience of some people. He didn't know ninety percent of what went on around his house, but I did. I mainly worked up around the yard, in the garden and all, and I got my eyes full more times than a few. He knew she was bad, but he didn't have any idea, not like I did, of how hard she rode her mama. I used to tell Ruby, I'd say, "No wonder Frances Hoover's a bitch." A man stays in the field all day, just comes in the house to eat and sleep, he's going to miss right much of what goes on. Then he'll look at his girl one day and she's swoll up with God knows whose baby and his wife's about to die for some attention, walking around trumped up all the time like she's the goddamn Queen of Sheba, and he'll just have to shake his head and walk right back out of the house and get on his tractor and plow that field, something he knows something about.

Lonnie Hoover was about as curious a man as you'll meet, curious man, strange man. You'd watch him take something and take it until you'd be about to bust open to go in and snatch what was going wrong out from under him and fix it, just get the damn thing fixed in a hurry. Like if you knew and he knew and everybody in the whole world knew somebody was regularly stealing out from his barns, and everybody knew exactly who was doing it, somebody right brazen, you'd see things gone and see things gone and wonder when in the hell Lonnie intended to do something about it. Or like if you knew who it was that took and borrowed a piece of machinery without telling somebody and then brought it back busted or just left it mired up in a field somewhere, you'd say, "When's Lonnie going to make his move, get his business back in order?" But he'd move so slow and quiet, and then after what seemed like forever, you'd see extra bags of fertilizer packed back up under the shelter or a brand new disk or mower pulled up beside the barn, and you'd say, "Well, it was about time," because you'd know Lonnie'd gone off somewhere with somebody and been made right with. Some quiet somewhere Lonnie and a man had sat in a truck and made arrangements for Lonnie to get back what was his, and usually more.

That's how he worked fixing Tiny Fran, old Tiny Fran dragging around like a slug, leaving a trail, something else Lonnie'd have to clean up. I remember one time a long time ago Ruby asked me why he hadn't just packed her up and put her away in somewhere to have that baby, or why he didn't pay a doctor off in town or somewhere under the counter to get rid of the whole business. Both of those quiet slipping around ways seemed to her like the way Lonnie liked to operate. But I said Lonnie was too sharp to fix something just for right now. He was thinking way on down the road. Get her wedged in. Clamp down on her. You get somebody like a Tiny Fran fixed up just for the here and now and it'd be silly and useless as finding the clown head up out of a Jack-in-the-box and shutting it back up inside and then leaving it out somewhere not thinking that the next one to come along will be bound to wind that thing up and watch it pop just for the pure fun of it. No, Lonnie intended to wedge her in, clamp down on her for the long haul.

Burr said he'd always remember how bright a day it was, how dry the dirt was deep down when he turned it up. He said that was what he had on his mind, all he was thinking of, the bright day and the dry dirt, and then he looked up down a row and saw Lonnie walking across the way to him. He said when he got to the end of the row he stopped the tractor, expecting to hear how Lonnie wanted him to do five more things before dark, but when the engine stopped Lonnie just squatted down and started handling a dirt clod and told Burr to get down, they needed to talk. Burr heard Lonnie out, all the "Boy, you might amount to something one day," and "You might could be somebody if you had something behind you. To be sure you don't want to work for farmers up and down this road the rest of your life." Burr heard him, listened hard, and what Lonnie said sounded reasonable, reasonable at least to a boy whose daddy and granddaddy and great-granddaddy had rented land from men like Lonnie and whose mama would die in a rocking chair, hemming dungarees, smelling like bleach and Argo starch. He just listened and agreed. "Marry Tiny Fran, whether you did it or not, just marry her and take a forty-eight-acre block, a good piece, drains good, not clay dirt, good loamy soil. Marry her and have something."

So what do you do? If she'd lived in town it could've been somebody saying "Marry the town whore and I'll give you Main Street, all up and down both sides, all the stores, all the things in the stores, Main Street." Burr said he didn't miss a beat. "I'll do it, Lonnie. I like Tiny Fran okay." But the fact was he thought the same about her everybody did. More times than a plenty I'd be out in the tractor yard with him and we'd see Tiny Fran go across the yard in something poured-on-looking and he'd do his made-up rhyme, "Between Franny's thighs is where her fanny lies, and that's what makes my britches rise." So you see, he didn't think she was okay. You generally don't marry somebody you feel like you can tease about like that. He wasn't a innocent lamb with blinders on, led, not knowing what all he might be in for with a girl like her. I just don't believe he had a clear idea how much and how long he'd have to pay. I always heard paybacks is hell.

Sorry as she was, though, I cannot honestly say I'd have turned her down if she'd been offered to me. That's a lot of property, and it's a lot of ways you can think up to stay out from under a woman, stay drunk, stay at work, stay in front of the television set.

But I did turn down one piece of property, Ruby's she

got when her parents died. I said, "I can't take it, Ruby. I can't take your land," and she said, "It's not mine!" I told her, "It's got your name on it," and she told me that was all that made it hers. I knew how she felt. She'd talked to me before. And it won't so much like I felt like I'd be cashing in on marrying somebody with some money, I'd wanted her before I knew what she'd come from. I just didn't want a place I didn't know. I know this place. Not taking the land was a choice I and Ruby had to make, and after we made it, we just had to close the door.

And I act like Burr was out there in that field with a choice, but he wasn't. He saw all that land he'd wanted and his daddy'd wanted and it wasn't a choice at all. That sun hitting the hill where his acres would start must've been the best-looking thing he'd ever seen, except for his dream woman, but she was in his head and she'd have to stay there.

Go ahead! Say how trading a happy life for land is foolish, how your peace of mind is more important than a piece of fertile land. But let me tell you this, when you grow up out here, when you know your family's been here long as theirs, meaning somebody like a Lonnie Hoover, when you know you can match time with them day for day, year for year, all this stretched out beside the road, back to the woods farther and farther, it pure hurts sometimes to look at it, looking at it after all that time you've spent with your face so close down on it over a bean row, touching it, turning it over, then going home to not one damn thing that's yours but some clothes and some pots and pans and a stick or two of furniture. You don't rent a boy a corner of a toy store, one down on that Main Street, and let him play all day until dark, every day, then send him home. No! You let him play a while, get attached to something, then say, "Take it, son. You can have it. You handled it enough. It's yours. It's right you should have it."

Let's say Burr's family rented from Lonnie's crowd a hundred years. That's a long time, especially when it looks to you like the whole rest of the world is drawing interest and all you're doing is putting in sweat and taking out the tired frustration. Then something comes along like Lonnie's bad situation that can end it and you and the rest of your line can have something, even if it is on account of what some teenage whore did one afternoon in the corncrib with God knows who or how many. That's one way of stopping what's gone on.

School's another way. Burr's girl, June, got a college degree, but what do you think would've been her chance if Burr hadn't told Lonnie he'd marry his girl? Not much. She'd have either been a Tiny Fran or swung back the other way around and been head over heels into the church down there and worried the pure living hell out of somebody wanting to witness all the time. Or she might would could've joined the 4-H and spent all her time dragging a calf around out here. But she got off from this place, had a mind to do something. You have to get off somewhere to do something makes some money. If she'd been born with her daddy still renting she'd still be here, and we'd all look at her all the time and think how that's a shame with her so smart.

No, you need something of your own, and you need it young so you can enjoy having it, not look back on all the work and wish you weren't so damn tired all the time with not a thing to show for it but your memory of working. But Burr was lucky, hard a time as he had managing Tiny Fran, he's told me he felt like he made out pretty good. He told me that a piece of something, the land, he's said what that gives a man is two things, some pride and some time, and you can sit back if you've a mind to and look outside and see all those folks hunched over picking, digging, pulling up out of your dirt, setting something back down in it, doing all the things you used to do, save for the grace of Lonnie Hoover.

He died this fall be ten years ago, lost the left side of his head then next thing you know he was gone. I told Ruby, I said, "I hate to say it, but I'll be glad to finally see what Lonnie has down in his will." I knew he had one, a man with as much business as he had has to. I don't. I'll die interstate, nothing to pass on and no heirs. Ruby's cancer ate up most of everything we had saved, and if it hadn't been for her brothers' picking up what they did, I don't think we'd have made it. Everything's so goddamn high. But I figured Lonnie'd have things squared away.

Sometimes I don't know why I think things, but I thought for damn sure he'd have sat in Lawyer Peele's office and said to him, "Well, I've got this one tenant been with my family long as I can remember, worked hard, never showed up drunk, never asked to borrow money, good man. I think I might let him have that piece he's been living on since he was born." And I thought if it didn't happen like that then he'd at least remember standing beside me in that field, and both of us boys, and seeing his daddy's tractor kill my daddy, kill him right out here in this field next to my house. Oh but hell no, neither thing counted.

Ruby'd tell me, "Try not to be bitter. Lonnie didn't know all you've been thinking." After she'd talk to me I'd feel better, and then her calming me down would wear off and I'd have to get out of the house and go out to the animal shelter and sit out there until I was so drunk I couldn't see straight, much less think.

See, it was I and daddy and Lonnie and his daddy, Henry, and all these farmers from up and down the road all standing at the edge of the field looking at Henry's new tractor. Nobody'd ever seen one except in the *Progressive Farmer*, and sure as hell couldn't afford one. But you can bet if it was big and new Henry'd beg, borrow, or steal for it. And there it was, big, red, and somebody said, "Show us what it'll do." Henry told daddy to hop up there and take it down a row. He'd been on it all morning so I didn't think anything of it. But what did bother me was Henry. See, he could've driven it himself, but what he was doing was he was letting daddy do it so he could stand there with all his buddies and see everything they were seeing, not just the new tractor, but the field and the tractor and a man he could say this and that to and order to manage both things for him. He was one white man that loved to watch another one work.

So daddy took the tractor down a row and Henry stood by us with his arms crossed and Lonnie stood next to him with his arms crossed just like his daddy's. And then daddy got to the other end and started to make a turn and I remember thinking, He's too close to the ditch, too close. Then the whole business turned over nice and easy like it was the most natural thing in this world for that tractor to fold over in that drainage ditch. We all ran down there but it wasn't a thing we could do, but I can still feel my arms ache for how hard I pulled at that tractor. Somebody pulled me away and told me, he said, "Only somebody mightier than us all could lift it," meaning God, and I felt like screaming right out in that field, "Is this how You treat the ones that love You?" My daddy might've been a sonofabitch sometimes, but he did evermore love the Lord.

But Lonnie didn't make things square and here I sit, old as the hills I farmed since I could hold a plow line, sitting here by myself, too. Land and children, they're the only things in this world that'll carry on for you, and here I am, going to my grave without either one.

8.

I've heard television evangelists say the Lord will return when you least expect him. I think I was afraid that same prophesy might've applied to John Woodrow those nights he didn't come home. I said to myself, About the time I get used to him being gone, when I've calmed down, returned the pistol, that'll be when he comes in, slobbering all over me, wanting to kiss and make up. Or either that'll be when the screen door blows open like almighty hell breaking loose and he'll come in pulling that dazed young girl behind him. And if and when push came to shove I saw myself pulling that pistol from under my pillow and saying, "So what do you think about little Miss Vanderbilt now?"

I remember I slept with my clothes on the three nights he was missing, and each morning before I went to the

Hoovers I'd change and take a little spit-bath, the kind mama would've only allowed if I was sick. It took me right many mornings of those baths to get past feeling guilty, like mama was standing in the door looking at me, holding a towel and some lavender soap, pointing the way to the tub. I can't remember exactly when it was but I can remember looking at my face in John Woodrow's old cracked up shaving mirror and saying out loud, "I'm doing the best I can." Lord, we will tell ourselves anything to get by. The best I could've done would've been to slip away while John Woodrow had slipped away, but planning, thinking about going home and facing mama and daddy became something I could only bear to think about right before I fell asleep at night, when your judgment's not good, that in-between time when you can make anything work as you'd please.

That third day I went to work was the day I met Jack. I was waiting under the big tree in the backyard, waiting for somebody, either Tiny Fran or her mother, to come out and tell me to come on in, you didn't dare just go up and knock on the door, be it front door or back door, and I saw a skinny man with his dungarees all hung down around his hips, swerving, trying to manage a tall load of manure, headed across the yard towards me.

He was forty then, but he looked ten years older. All that time out in the sun had dried and pulled his skin. He says he's never minded it, that he's not what he calls a town man, trying to stay young and fresh despite the odds. He's always said it's fine for women to trick time with lotions and what-not because a trick pulled off just right, he says, is really something to look at, smell of, touch. I know he's referring to me. I know I'm every bit of his experience.

But he pushed his wheelbarrow right up to me that day like approaching young women waiting under pecan trees was something he did every day, like it was something he regularly did on the way from the chicken house to the garden. I wasn't afraid at all by the way he looked at me, not like the way I felt when I'd stand up from picking and see the crew chief staring. Jack's look was more like what happens when I'm walking from here to the store and the sun catches something on the side of the road just right, and I wonder if it's a dime or a piece of jewelry, but then I know nobody out here has any jewelry to lose, so I pick the dime up, rub the dirt off, look at it hard, hard as I'd look if it'd been a brooch, just because I'd found it, and finding anything of value is unusual, be it a dime or a man with clay-red skin or a young woman resting under a pecan tree.

And this is the first thing my husband ever said to me. He said, "This is something. You smoking a cigarette and it ninety-some-odd degrees out here." He can burn right through to the heart of a thing. But I'd about had it with men and their opinions of me so I told him it was my business how hot I was. Then he set the load down and said to me, "Well, if it's your business, I reckon it's your business." I just smoked my cigarette and watched him. I thought he was sure to say something else just as curious.

He stood there and watched me too, and then he wanted to know who I was, what I was doing under Lonnie's tree, how long I'd been there, if I was with the migrants, and if I was married. He got all those questions out before I could think up answers to any. I told him the truth to everything except the migrant question. I said I was travelling with them doing research. I think he knew I was lying, but he didn't say anything, and he never has.

After I answered the question about being married, he wanted to know who to, and I told him, and that was a dead giveaway. But I didn't back down. I just hoped he wouldn't ask me anything else. I said, "I'm married to John Woodrow. He's one of the workers, but see, I met him at the beginning of my research. He's a great help with my work." The more I talked, the deeper in I got. When I stopped he thought for a minute and said, "John Woodrow. He's that one they found cut up last night."

You can't imagine what was going through my head. I told him to tell me everything he knew. He said it might upset me, but I told him to please go on and tell me. So he told me Lonnie had gotten a call late the night before from the sheriff, and that he'd had to get up and go to town, to the hospital and the jailhouse. Apparently, what happened was John Woodrow left that girl and her baby somewhere and got up with some of his drinking buddies, the sorriest of the sorriest, as Jack would call them, and they all went to a pool hall in town, and one thing led to another and they all got in a drunk fight with some other sorriness and when all was said and done, one was in jail, one was missing, and John Woodrow was in the hospital. The sheriff figured they were migrants, and he knew Lonnie had just gotten a new crew in, so he called him, and sure enough, they were his. He said word wasn't out yet, that the crew chief probably didn't know, more than likely wouldn't care. He said Lonnie wouldn't have cared except that it aggravated him to have to get up and go to town in the middle of the night.

Jack also told me I should come to his house if I needed him for anything, and he pointed it out to me across the field. When he said "needed" and "anything" I knew he meant food, money, somewhere to rest awhile. And then he told me his name, his whole name the way he enjoys saying it, "stokes the fire, stokes the stove, stokes the fiery furnace of hell!"

Tiny Fran interrupted us, calling me inside to find her blessed crackers, and at first I thought she might have something nasty to say about John Woodrow being hurt, but then I realized she wouldn't associate me with the mess at all, if her daddy'd even mentioned it in the house. I didn't have a last name there. I was either just Ruby or "that girl." So I decided to use that time of nobody knowing to rest in and gather up what strength I'd need when everything came at me, when all those workers would turn their petty curiosity on me. I just turned it all off. All I'd ever heard from John Woodrow was how ignorant I was, so I said, Fine, I'm ignorant of the fix he's in.

I knew if he was able to speak he was cursing me to anybody who'd listen, cursing that daddy's girl he'd married and thinks she's too good to come help the man who took her away from all that and tried to make a hardworking, honest-to-God, common, everyday woman out of her, "Put some meat on them bones!" My ears rang for hearing him say that. And all I could've said back to him was, "That's exactly what happened, nail on the head. Bleed, John Woodrow, bleed."

Word of his injury soon travelled up one tobacco row and down the next, and by the time the workers came up into the yard that afternoon it seemed like every one of them knew exactly how many stitches he'd had, how deep the cuts were, and how his lung was punctured in such-and-such a place. Walking to the house after work, a woman who'd never spoken to me before came up and patted my arm and said, "I hear your man got cut real bad, might not make it." She waited for me to touch her back or maybe break down, but I didn't. I was so ticked off all I could say to her was, "That's what they tell me." She snapped her hand off me and told me it seemed like a woman would stand by her man, irregardless, and it seemed like that woman would be especially true after something like this, irregardless. I guess she meant regardless of the fact that he was a known bastard. But she broke stride with me and fell in with her friends, and I could hear her tell them how insensitive I was and with John Woodrow "laid up in the hospital, cut up and about to hardly make it." Then one of the women said that was a shame, and she proceeded to tell them about how her sister nursed her husband after a bad wreck last year. She said the man's face was sliced this way and that and his wife stayed right by him, feeding him through a straw, picking glass slivers from his lips. The woman told the story like it was a privilege for the man's wife to pick at his lips. And I know they also thought I'd be doing the wifely thing to sit by John Woodrow and swab his wounds just because, all because he was my man. I'd nurse Jack all day and all night, but that's a different story.

And while they walked on I slipped back and crossed a wide ditch and stood on the edge of the wheat field, wondering if I should wade across to Jack's house. But I didn't go. I just stayed on the edge there and looked at his house, this house. I had no idea it'd be my house five months from then. And after a long time of purely standing and staring, wondering about my whole big mess, I crossed back over the ditch and went home. When I got there I found the pistol and put it at the bottom of my bag, way down under where my lingerie had been. I'd never see those nice things again, but I still hear the pistol.

That night after I'd eaten supper Jack came to see me. I remember him standing at the screen door, and I could smell him. He smelled like soap, a sweet soap. And he said, "I hate to be the one to have to tell you, but your husband passed a little while ago." He paused a minute, and then he said, "It was the lungs. They wouldn't stay up is what Lonnie told me." And the very next thought I had was how I was alone, not John Woodrow's dead, ding-dong John Woodrow's dead. I was glad to have Jack stay there with me while I cried everything out of my system.

Sometimes I think the smart thing to have done then would've been to pack right up and go home, fast as I could, call daddy and have him come for me. But I couldn't. I hadn't just stayed out all night and was nervous about walking into breakfast. This wasn't anything like that, like knowing that everything would blow over by lunch and by dinnertime you'd be one of them again, forgiven, everything back in its place, including you. Where was my place there? I wasn't a son, not a boy who could come home and fall into plowing or mowing a field and earn his way back into his home. I was a daughter who'd mainly watched men work a farm from a kitchen window.

When mama and daddy died and everything passed to Paul and Jimmy and me, I let them divide my part between them. It wasn't so much that they'd worked the place and I hadn't, they'd known the value of it. They'd always known what we had there. Before I did it though, I talked it over with Jack and told him if he really wanted me to I could keep my land and we could move there together and work it. Then he'd have something. He's always wanted something. But he told me he couldn't take it, he appreciated the offer but he couldn't take a strange place. I should've known better than to offer it. He wanted, still wants land, but not any land will do. He'd hoped for this place but I'm afraid that hope died with Lonnie.

And I can't even say I did my part inside, the woman's work, and let the men manage the outside. But I wasn't helpless, just useless. See, I had it in the back of my mind that one day I'd have somebody like Sudie Bee to help me, and I'd be able to pass for a grown woman, or the lady of the house. Somebody like Sudie Bee covers for people. Having her in my kitchen would've been no different from those commercials you see where the husband says, "Mmm, Mmm, this sure is good cake. Tastes like you made it from scratch," and the wife just winks at the camera and wiggles the mix box behind her back. It's not any different from that at all.

Mama'd baste a turkey that Sudie Bee had chased, caught, killed, scalded, everything. She'd tap more salt into the pan dressing Sudie Bee had made, and I'd come in when everything was basted, salted, and garnish the turkey, put the napkins in rings. I put finishing touches on mama's finishing touches. I was twice-removed from the real work, far away from mama stooped over a roasting pan brushing butter on the turkey, and even farther away from Sudie Bee running around the chicken yard with an ax in her hand. But I had it in the back of my mind that mama was capable of doing all Sudie Bee's jobs, and she just didn't do them because she needed to be free to do other things, like sitting down at the kitchen table every morning with her cup of tea and a notepad, making a list for the day, then going upstairs to bathe, read, rest, embroider, then coming back downstairs to check on how things were moving along, do some of her finishing touches and split a RC Cola with Sudie Bee.

Try as I might, I'll never forget the first night I spent with John Woodrow in one of those little migrant places, and I opened up two kinds of canned something and stirred everything together in one pot. I stood at that grimey old hot plate and wished Sudie Bee would come through the back door, take her hat off, come over to me, take the spoon out of my hand and say, "Lord have mercy! You got to stir it quicker than that to keep it from ruining all on the bottom. Let me do it. You go set the table and put the ice in the glasses." But she didn't show up to keep me from ruining the food, and I doubt we had any ice for the glasses.

I spent many a frustrating hour learning how to cook, trying to remember how Sudie Bee had done things, but mostly making things up as I went along. Poor Jack had to choke down a few dry mouthfuls before I could even make a recipe come out. Cooking's not like cleaning. You don't just know what good is and then cook it. You need a touch that comes with time and patience, especially if you grew up playing the piano while meals were being prepared and then coming into the kitchen just in time to put parsley on the plates. But you ought to see the way I've kept this house and cooked for Jack. I'm sorry to say that I might not have much in my life to be proud of, but I'm surely pleased with myself every time I see bread rise, and it rises every time.

I don't hear any more shots. He's finished. I have to be, too, for now. Some times it's easier to stop thinking about things than others, but then how many people do you know who're able to get off a loop as easily as they got on it? Daydreaming, loving the wrong man, smoking, all habits hard to break.

9.

The night before Burr and Tiny Fran got married I didn't sleep not one wink, worrying, worrying, worrying. I worried about it all. I ought to've slept though, as hard as Frances'd run me all week. "Do this. Do that." Kept me busy as a one-arm paper hanger, pruning the hedgebushes, arranging pine straw, cleaning out the chicken house. By the time Saturday rolled around I was so tired I thought I might liable not to be able to stand up for Burr, but I did. Pissed Frances off too, me standing up front at the wedding. I know it did. But I didn't give a whit. That was I and Burr's business. He's like a son to me.

About all I had to look forward to at that wedding, besides being Burr's best man, was seeing Ruby. We'd been hanging right tight since John Woodrow died. It wasn't anybody else there I gave a happy hurrah about, like all Frances's out-of-town family. They didn't have the slightest notion what was going on that day. Burr told me they had the impression him and Tiny Fran had been courting a fair amount of time. Now I wonder where they got that? I wanted to say to Frances, I wanted to ask her, "You really think you're slick, don't you? Here you are trying to pull the wool over somebody's eyes." I guess she thought shaking Tiny Fran's pooched-out self into that shift-looking dress, and it white, would fool her folks. But I thought, Frances, you just wait till nigh about five months from now and here's Tiny Fran and a teeny baby and see if they don't start counting on their fingers.

And you can damn well bet old preacher what's-his-face from down at Ephesus wouldn't have anything to do with it. He'd gotten wind of the mess from somebody at Porter's store and he wasn't touching it. They had to bring in a civil somebody. And I could've put another dollar down on Burr's mama and daddy not showing up. I know they both stayed shut up in the house all day, his daddy probably worrying the tar out of Burr the whole time he was trying to get his clothes on.

Burr's daddy, Leon, was a mealy-mouth sonofabitch if there ever was one, same age as me, always treated me like I didn't have enough sense to pour piss out of a boot with the instructions on the heel. He'd go around out here with his big old cigar in his mouth, smiling like Franklin D. Roosevelt, acting he was happy as he could be to be a poor dumb old working man, but you knew it was the opposite true. Then he'd go home at night and beat his wife, beat Burr too. And then poor Pansy died like she did, up sewing in the middle of the night.

Used to he used to go sit at the store, rear back, rub that great big belly of his and say, "Well, I'll tell you, I might be just a poor old working man, but I've got the sense to see Lonnie Hoover might ought to sell that hay for a dime more a bale if he expects to turn a profit on it," or "Nobody's going to ask me what I think about it, me being just a poor working man, but if they did I'd tell them Lonnie might ought not to plant that back field with fescue again this year." You wanted to say to him, "That's right. Nobody gives a damn what you think, so shut up," but it wasn't worth the air. You just rolled your eyes. And then his only boy marries a Hoover and gets that back field and now he's one of the ones that's not going to ask Leon his opinion.

After Burr got married I remember how Leon had his heart attack and they laid him out. I went with Burr and stood there with him looking in the casket and he told me, he said, "All my daddy ever wanted was a nice suit of clothes, a fine automobile, and some respect." Burr'd bought a hundred-and-fifty-dollar suit to bury him in. Leon would've set fire to it if Burr'd offered it to him while he was living, bad as his mouth would've been watering for it. And then I and Burr went to the Buick place and he got a little model automobile and went back to the funeral home, slipped it in beside Leon where nobody'd spot it and have a time with it. Then I said to Burr, "Burr, he's got the fine suit of clothes and a brand new Buick, I guess a nice service'll have to do for the respect." Then he told me his daddy got respect, he knew he'd gotten it because it was something he'd beat him into telling him all the whole time he was growing up. No wonder he didn't go to the boy's wedding. He must've been pure eat up with jealousy.

But on back, I got to the house and Ruby was running a dustrag in the living room, and I asked her how about if we went to my house and cooked supper after all the commotion was over. She was just learning how to cook then and she liked to try out things on me. But while we were standing there we heard Frances in the next room telling Lonnie how that little girl in there, meaning Ruby, wanted to act like she was better than somebody, said she'd snubbed her when she'd tried to show her how to arrange some little pick-up sandwiches on a tray. Then Lonnie said, all he said to her was, "I told you you should've hired a nigger."

I said right out loud, "Lord God Almighty." I knew what Ruby'd come from by then, how her daddy was a Ruritan, and I just wanted to grab her and tell her something, but I didn't feel like I could touch her. She just looked down at her feet and she didn't say anything for a minute, then she started giggling, had to pure hold the dustrag up to her mouth to stop up the sound. I said, "What's so funny?" I sure didn't see anything funny. And she said, "Whew! I just thought of Frances tasting one of those little lady-fingers her sister brought and commenting on how she put in way, way too much salt. Then I say maybe she ought to have something to wash it down, how it's the rat poison I sprinkled on top that brings out the salty flavor. And then Frances grabs at her throat and falls out."

I thought Ruby'd lost her mind! I'd never heard of such from a woman, but that was before I knew how to take her. Sometimes she'd fool you, funny when she meant to be serious and the other way around. I got in hot water many a time not taking Ruby the way she wanted me to. Yes, I sure thought she was thinking about doing something to old Frances. That was also before she told me what she'd had lined up for John Woodrow. After then I always said, You better think twice before you step on Ruby's toes. I remember one time we were joking around having a good time and I asked her, "What kind of punishment you got in mind for me if I step out of line?" And do you know what she said? She said, "Oh, I'm going to love you to pieces, love you to death." How about that? Hear such as that for twenty-five years and see don't you miss it when it's gone. It's a cold, cold heart that wouldn't.

10.

J ack came in the house, kissed me like I knew he
would. Now he's gone again, gone down to the store
to meet his pinball game. I should've gone with him. I
usually do. I just didn't think I'd be much fun today, and
even a short walk seems to ruin me lately.

I wonder what mama would have to say about me sitting here alone as I am, waiting for Jack's pinball game to
break up, no friends to speak of, except Burr and June, my
brothers and their families. I bet she'd want to know if I
could say I'm happy in spite of everything, living so far
out here, being sick. She'd say, "Tell me, has there been a
single ounce of good to come of all you've been through?"

I'd look around the house, far as I can see from this
kitchen table, while mama waits for an answer, and I'd
show her Jack's old brogans in the corner by the broom,

the picture of a snowman June made for me that Jack had framed, photographs I brought back when I went home for daddy's funeral, especially the one of me holding my little prize Schubert bust at my ten-year piano recital, and then I'd say, "Well, mama, I do believe I am. In spite of everything, I do believe I've been happy. That John Woodrow time was something I went through to get where I am, and I can appreciate good now because of it." Surely that would satisfy her.

June's been about as much reason for the good I've felt as any other, all those times she'd run to Jack and me. I couldn't count how many mornings we got up and found her sitting on our front porch, swinging, waiting for us to start stirring, Saturdays, summer days, school holidays. She still comes to see us about every other weekend. I've been making some clothes for her to take on a cruise this winter.

Since I've been sick June's brought me a present every time she's visited. I've told her not to bring me anything, but I feel like I have to accept the things, and when she leaves I take the robes and gowns and slippers, they're all so pretty and I know expensive, and I put them in the cedar chest with all the presents she made me when she was small. Sometimes I can't help but think how mama would've liked June.

Jack and I'd been married about three years with no

babies when we figured something might really be wrong. It took us another year to decide to see a doctor and then another year to get enough nerve to go. When we finally went and found out I wasn't likely to ever have a child, I think Jack and I both more or less assumed possession of June. Burr knew what we were doing. It didn't bother him. I think he was glad for the help with her. A man must have a hard time looking after a girl.

I'll never forget her coming here once when she was twelve, crying, scared to death, absolutely no idea what had happened to her. I talked to her, explained things the best I could, and let her spend the rest of the afternoon here with me. Later on, I walked her back home and I got Tiny Fran out on the porch and asked her why, why for goodness sakes she hadn't talked to the girl about her body, why she at least hadn't gotten her some books to read. Tiny Fran told me it was none of my business, got pretty belligerent about it. We went around and around on the subject of her irresponsibility until I just gave up. By then I should've known better than expect her to apologize for the past or change so the future'd be different, better. But I went right back in the house and helped June pack an overnight bag, marched right past Tiny Fran with her, and brought her back here. Burr came over later that day and after I told him what had happened, he gave June some money to buy a dress she'd had her eye on. I promised her we'd go into town and get it when Jack got home. Burr thanked me for looking after her, bringing her back with me. We were both surprised Tiny Fran let me take her without another fight, but you never really could predict her. Nobody predicted she'd leave him. We all thought she'd stay out here chipping away at everybody's peace of mind as long as she lived.

If Tiny Fran felt pushed hard enough she'd even say Jack and I brainwashed June. When June was small and Tiny Fran would say something like that with Burr present, he'd wear himself out trying to explain how ridiculous she was being. He'd bring up all those times she'd jumped all over June for no reason, humiliated her, and he'd come in from the fields to find June crying on the steps or shut up in her room. Then Burr got tired of listening to her and tired of running down his list, and when she'd get on one of her screaming jags he'd just bring June to me and ask me to keep her until he could get Tiny Fran in order. And more nights than a few, Burr himself spent the night on our couch. Poor Burr was certainly caught between a rock and a hard place with his wife and the land her daddy gave him. And when the two children got caught in the middle, Roland was pushed to lie, steal, and hurt anything he touched, and June, thank goodness, was pushed to me, straight across her daddy's field to me.

It took everything Tiny Fran had to act civil towards

me, and when she was, there was a catch to it, something behind it, like the time they needed to go stay with her mother during an operation and she called over here, cordial, friendly as she could be. I kept wanting to say, "Get to the point, Tiny Fran, go ahead and get to the point." And when she finally did she told me she wanted to know if Jack and I could look after June and Roland the week she and Burr would be gone. I knew that by then she'd called everybody she knew and they'd all said the same thing I was about to tell her, "June, fine, but I can't handle Roland. I just can't handle him." He was too wild. I couldn't control him. They ended up having to take Roland with them, leaving June here. She was six then.

I can't think of anything in the world, outside of a very good, very long dream, to compare that week with her to. I've not had another one like it. We'd all get up in the morning, play, have lunch, play some more, eat dinner, play. I'd have to nudge Jack out the door to go over to Burr's and keep things running, keep the help busy. He said he'd rather stay here with us and weave potholders, and I believed him. She slept in the back bedroom with puppies she'd sneak out of the pen out back and turn into the house. Jack would wake me up in the middle of the night and tell me to go in there and look at the baby asleep in a bedful of dogs.

When Burr came to get her he came in the kitchen and

sat down by her and asked her if she'd had a good time. She wouldn't answer. I told her to tell her daddy what all we'd done, maybe show him some of the potholders we'd made. But she wouldn't speak. She wouldn't even look at him for rolling her fists around in her eyes, shuffling her feet, shrugging when he touched her. I told her she should be sweet and he'd let her come and stay again, but I knew how she felt. I didn't want to be sweet myself. Jack couldn't watch her go. When he'd seen Burr driving up in the yard he went to the bathroom and told me to tell him he was tied up and would see him later that day.

Some childless couples, my brother and his wife for one, get along by pretending that their dog or cat is a member of the family. And it's all over television, all the money people are willing to spend on fancy pet food. Jack and I had sat here many a night laughing about a woman we saw at the bank who had her little poodle dressed in a Santa Claus suit. But we couldn't say anything anymore, not after the way we behaved when June left.

We were out in the yard not more than two days later, weeding, patching up the dog pen, and I noticed Jack over in the big circle Prince Albert ran around in. He had the dog up on his hind paws, holding his front ones, making him dance a little jig. Prince Albert was so old and floppy by then he just went along. Jack even called out for me to look at the dog dancing. And it wouldn't be right if I didn't tell the rest of it. I ran inside and got my Brownie and took half a roll of film of Jack making the dog dance. After all that Jack walked to the store and came back with canned dog food, and he went inside and came back out with it all scooped out in a good dish. While Prince Albert ate Jack explained to me about how nutritious the real meat chunks were, and I couldn't help but think about how many times I'd reminded Jack to put a little spigot water in with that dry, cheap old dog chow, and how he'd told me gravy'll take the edge off a dog. And there he was, throwing this old dog a little party.

And we kept on, and it got worse. Jack would try his baseball hat on Prince Albert's head and I'd break my neck trying to get inside and get the camera before he lost that pose. Jack would come and stand over me fixing a roast or something and tell me to save a good piece, not to pepper it too much. And we were even sillier over the puppies, sitting on the back steps, looking at them rolling around in the pen, wondering what sort of dogs they'd grow up to be.

But all that stopped when we got the film developed. I thought we would've been happy to go over it all again, but all the pictures did was show us how badly we wished it was a baby in a highchair, birthday cake all over her face, not our half-deaf, half-blind dog slobbering all over a good piece of shoulder roast, licking one of my blue flowered plates.

We looked at all the pictures and then put the envelope away. I run across it every now and then but I've not opened it up. I don't need to, knowing what's in it, knowing what's not in it. The next time June visited us I took just as many pictures of her, and I kept on taking them. Those I don't mind looking at. I can stare at those long enough to see what I want to, see her mine. It's just a matter of seeing what you want to see. People do it with hearing, thinking, and saying all the time. But seeing's harder, especially when you know that an old bulldog is never going to get you confused with her mama, but a little girl might. If you stay by her, she might.

II.

Burr told me last week, he said to me, "The years my wife's been gone have been the happiest years of my life." He said all he missed about her leaving was wishing she'd go. I told him it was a shame in this world he couldn't have had a woman like Ruby, and he just had to shake his head like "I know."

Tiny Fran left him right after June went off to college. I was out sweeping under the pony shelter and he showed up and said to me, "Well, she left." He said they'd had a royal knock-down drag-out over how much money he'd been mailing to June, and one thing led to another and she got her suitcase out and what she didn't cram in it she threw at him. Then he asked her what she was going to live on and she told him she'd borrow on or sell off her part of the farm and that'd keep her fairly well. Burr said he thought, Oh, hell no you won't. And he went and got his checkbook and bought her out right there, wrote out something and she signed it. I said, "Well, congratulations, let's take a drink." He said he could use one. He needed more than one, that's for damn sure. I told him I'd be interested to see how long the money held out. He said that'd depend on how many times she walked by a shoe store. And sure enough, last year about this time she called him and said she was in a bind, and every month since then he's been sending her a check. Ruby told him it was the best investment he ever made, that maybe she'd fall in love with a shoe salesman. We all had to laugh.

Ruby loved Burr and June, tolerated Tiny Fran, but pure couldn't stomach Roland. From the time Roland was born until the time they led him off away from out here Tiny Fran stayed right on top of him like she was the hen and he was the damn egg, just raising all grades of hell if anybody came near him. You'd go up in the yard and she'd be hanging out the wash, him pulling on her skirt and whining, and you'd hear her saying, "Mama'll make you a big old cake soon as she's done." They'd sit down and split a chocolate cake but she wouldn't have given June air if she was in a jug. June'd have to come over here to have a treat. Roland wouldn't have anything to do with us, least not until he came and killed Ruby's mule. Before that, Ruby'd say, "Well, Roland's like he is because his mama keeps him so close, and you might not want to excuse him but you can see why he's a problem." Then after the mule Ruby had to stop making a allowance for him. You'd see her tighten up when somebody talked about him.

June turned out though, I and Burr and Ruby jumping in between her and Tiny Fran every time she tried to ruin her. She's a architect in town now. I still get to see her right much. You won't see Roland though. He's in jail they said for at least ten years. And I'll tell you what, I think it ought to be ten hundred years.

Listen and let me tell what else I think about it. Listen to how God up there is supposed to make everything and everybody and everything's due to turn out according to his will and all. And we get the wars and the people starving and people hurting people and animals the way Roland did, and I'm supposed to go down there to Ephesus on a Sunday morning and say, "Thank you, Jesus, thank you for the sunshine and the food on my table and all the birds singing and the likes of Adolf Hitler and Roland Stanley." No thank you! I'll have no part of it! Beats the hell out of me why somebody'd want to sit up somewhere and think up harm, start it to going, then say, "Oh, let me make it up to you. Here's this rainbow so you can remember how I can kill everything and everybody, but I swear I won't again." How would you like it if I slammed your fingers in the car door and then watched you standing there holding your hand and it throbbing and turning blue, and I said, "Oh, let me make it up to you. Here's a quarter and I promise I won't ever do it again"? How good do you think you'd be listening to somebody then, especially somebody who ought to be hustling you in the car to take to the doctor, not giving you a quarter to hold in a busted up hand? I think about that and want to tell it to Cecil Spangler and every other gung-ho Christian that's been out here trying to save me, and then I'd say, "Think about that, O ye of all that faith!"

More than one time when Tiny Fran's heard me comment on the way she handled her children, especially Roland, she's said, "How come you can profess to know so much and you and Ruby can't even have any babies? Who made you the expert?" I used to tell her I and Ruby had the instinct for it whereas she'd be better off with billy goats and guinea pigs. Burr used to hear us going at it like that and laugh his head off.

Tiny Fran was known for showing her tail, but she couldn't just show it, then you'd laugh, and that'd be all until the next time she'd do something ignorant. No, half the time she'd fairly well stun you with something so ugly you'd have to say to yourself, I cannot believe that came out of a human being, like at the beach one time, like with Ruby this summer be eighteen years ago.

It was hot and summer like it is now and Burr came over

here late in the day and asked me why I and Ruby didn't ride to the coast with them the next weekend. He said Tiny Fran threw a natural-born fit over the idea but June threw a bigger one over the idea of us not, and you can bet which one Burr went along with. I told him we'd go, long as Tiny Fran stayed away from Ruby and didn't bother her. He said he'd do his best to keep the lid on her.

We went all crammed into Burr's car, and before we'd backed out of the driveway I wished we'd put Roland in the damn trunk. I know he was just six and you're supposed to make a allowance for them that young, but you tell that to somebody that's not shut up in a car with a damn demon child and his mama.

When we got going Ruby kept trying to be friendly and pleasant, talking about how nice it was to be going to the beach and so forth and so on. I can still see her riding the whole way with a pineapple cake between her feet and holding a pound cake. Then it started to be every single time Ruby'd open her mouth to say something Tiny Fran'd cut in, irked me so bad. Finally Burr told her to let Ruby finish a sentence. That made her so mad she twisted and got herself up on one thigh and rode the rest of the trip with everything pushed into the door, looking like she was looking out the window. We even stopped and all of us but her got out to get a hamburger, and I thought, Stew then, stay mad, my dogs wouldn't sit in a car with it this hot.

I know she was about parched but she'd have swallowed poison before she'd have got out and had a mouthful to eat with us.

The rest of the way Tiny Fran sucked her breaths in and blew them out like she was having to strain for air, huffing and puffing, hot with all of us. Then Burr told her just to keep on like that and she'd have a real fine time that weekend, if she didn't make herself pass out before we got there. Then he went on into how he intended to enjoy himself that weekend, fishing, relaxing, flying a kite, watching the young girls. Then she said something. She said, "What do you intend for me to be doing while all that's going on?" He said it was plenty she could do, play with the children, go all through the shell shops with Ruby, play miniature golf, go down the strip to the little amusement park and have her weight guessed. I thought I was going to fold over laughing on Ruby when he said that. Then she told him to go to hell, said that applied to everybody. I know Ruby hated to laugh at a woman making a ass out of herself, but you couldn't help it. You just couldn't.

We finally got there and we pulled up at the Pettigrew's Cottages. I remember it was Pettigrew's because I couldn't imagine somebody being named something something Pettigrew. I can't picture a Pettigrew. But we pulled up and I leaned over to Ruby and I said, "I thought we were staying at a motel. These are just shacks!" She said it didn't matter as long as they were clean. And Lord was it hot! Hotter than forty hells, not enough breeze to do any good.

After we got everything unloaded and inside, Burr told me to let's get the fishing mess ready and go buy some bait and go on out. Then listen and tell me if you hear something funny. Tiny Fran broke in and asked him where he'd put the folding chairs, and Burr said, "What?" and she said, "You know, my brand new folding chairs I got especially for this trip." Burr told her he didn't remember packing or unpacking them and he went on about his business. Then she got hot, she yelled at him, "Well, what do you expect me to sit on?" Then listen, he said, "I guess you can sit down on your fist and lean back on your thumb!" I laughed and Ruby laughed and I thought Burr was going to choke he laughed so hard. Tiny Fran told us all to go to hell and went on inside.

Then we all went out to see the water, stayed out there about all afternoon. I wore some Bermuda shorts Ruby'd got me when she bought her bathing suit. I said she could take the matched T-shirt back to the store. She'd gotten a idea I'd look good in red, but I told her to take it on back, I'd wear a undershirt. You ought to have seen Ruby. She was the one who looked like something in red, red top with a blue bottom, two-pieced. She was only twenty-seven then and her skin still snapped back like a rubber band. Tiny Fran getting into her feed sack of a bathing suit must've been like cramming mud in a glove.

Well, when the sun was cooling down Burr said he guessed we'd all better get on back up to the house, that the children looked about played out, and he knew Ruby must be tired of chasing them. Then he called out and asked Tiny Fran what she had on the menu. She looked up, looked like a turtle pulling his head up, and she said she was on vacation and that folks could fend for themselves tonight.

He told her, he said, "If you can't find the energy to cook then I guess you can't get fixed up to go out somewhere either. You just lay around here and we'll tell you how good it was." She told him to go on and leave her alone and she heaved herself up on one side and plopped over to get some sunshine on that big white stomach of hers. That was one woman that had no business in a bathing suit. But we all went in and left her out there baking and not more than fifteen minutes later here she comes, stomping across the sand dunes, scared to death she might miss a meal.

She walked right by us all on the porch, took Roland inside with her though. He had a earful to give her about June throwing sand on him, and when I heard it I thought, Bullshit! It was the other way around! We could hear him whining to her inside there and Ruby just tried to talk over it, telling June how she ought to wear this or that pretty outfit to the restaurant.

Then we all went in, sat around talking, and Ruby said, "Where's June?" I thought she was still out on the porch, but Ruby looked out the door and said, "No, she's not on the porch." Then we heard it, sounded like somebody was pure cutting somebody open back there, and then you heard Tiny Fran say, "June, you give that horn back to him right this damn minute," and then you heard June say, "I had it first." And then here comes June tearing down the hall with a plastic trumpet in her mouth, running I know straight for Ruby, and then here comes Roland behind her and he tackles her from the behind and there goes June. Tiny Fran came behind Roland and yelled at June, she said, "I told you to give that baby his horn!" That baby, and him two years older than her. But there June was face down and just gagging and gurgling and Ruby went and bent down beside her, turned her over and took and used her skirt to get the blood off her face. She told Burr to get some ice real quick, and then she looked in June's mouth and said the blood probably made it look worse than it was but she ought to go to the emergency room anyway. Then Tiny Fran told Roland to go back in the bedroom and she got right next to Ruby, Ruby still wiping blood and trying to calm June down, and she said, "Move! Get your goddamn claws off her!" It came out roaring, scared Ruby so bad she started shaking. I told her to shut her nasty mouth or I'd show her the back of my hand. She told me I was the one that needed to shut up, and then Ruby said we didn't need a fight and all. Burr came in with the ice and told Tiny Fran to straighten up and go pull the car around, and when she did I and Burr laid June in the back seat and him and her and Roland took her to the hospital. I'd have said we wanted to go but I figured we weren't family, and Ruby'd been made to feel in the way enough for one day.

Ruby went in a bedroom and laid across the bed. I stood in the door watching her. She told me to come on in and lay down, that the bed was cool and it was finally a breeze starting to blow in the window. I did, and then she told me to hold her real tight from the back. We laid there until way after it got dark, and she cried most of the time.

I knew Ruby. I knew she was crying for babies she wished had been born to us, ones I couldn't give her. And as ignorant a man as I am, I knew what I was hearing. I knew the sound of Ruby crying for babies the way I know a robin's call, the same way I know the sparrows'.

Ruby'd tell me she knew it was her fault, how it was more than likely something John Woodrow gave her that got in the way of us having a child. But I couldn't believe it was her fault and not mine. See, usually if it was something wrong going on it was me that caused it. And it was. But the doctor said it just happens sometimes, and you can't lay blame. I said, "Well, fix it!" But he said it won't no fix to it. I looked over and looked at Ruby. She said it was okay.

I thought about getting a orphan, like asking Ruth Hartley if we couldn't take and raise one of the little girls she was bringing up, but when I saw how June was taking up with Ruby I decided to wait and see if she couldn't fill in. She never did all the way but she did some. I really didn't want to try out for a orphan. All Ruby would've needed would've been for the state to tell her I wasn't right, not enough money or sense to trust a child with.

I sit here acting like if I and Ruby had had a child it'd have turned out like June, good, smart, but that's an awful lot to pretend like what might would could've happened. I know everybody that wants a child sits around and thinks up a good boy or girl skipping rope, licking a ice cream cone. No, you're going to get some bad. You just don't want to be the one that gets stuck raising it.

Somebody bad like Roland, all he's ever after is wanting to watch somebody suffer, like the way he made Ruby and her anniversary mule suffer. I remember when his mess finally caught up with him and they put him in the jailhouse, I thought, They ought to do the same thing to him he did to the mule. You'll never hear of such as what happened to Sugar Pete. I think of it now and say, Poor old mule.

It was one weekend I and Ruby left here and went to the mountains to visit Jimmy and his wife and her other brother, Paul. Before we left I went over yonder and asked Burr if he'd look after things around here, feed up, keep the mail picked up, and he said he would so I said we'd go on then. We went and had a good time, and when we got home the first thing I and Ruby did was to go out to the pony barn and check on her mule. I'd just given it to her for a anniversary because she'd said she wanted something to ride on along beside me when I'd take a pony down the path, something slow she felt like wouldn't get out from under her. So I got her a mule, and she was tickled.

But that Sunday morning late we walked out to the pony barn and went under the shelter and I had to holler, "Don't look, Ruby! Stay back!" But she looked in, looked up at him swinging, all swoll, and she just had to sit down on the feedbox and cry. I felt like I pure had to hit somebody. I said, "I know who did it! He can't hide! Goddamn you, Roland Stanley!"

Ruby told me I ought not to swear at Roland like that unless I knew for sure he was the one did it. She wanted to know how I didn't know it wasn't some of the Mexican boys Luther Snipes had picking cucumbers.

I said to her, "Ruby, you don't know people like I do." I said, "Mexicans would've drove up out here drunk, took Sugar Pete for a little ride up and down the path, put her back, and wouldn't have left a thing to tell it by but beer bottles." I told her a mean wild-ass boy like Roland that ought to know better is the kind that'll hang a mule.

Then she wanted to know what we ought to do next, and I told her just to go on back to the house and let me take care of it. And I did. I went right across the field to Burr's house and went right on in the door, and I told them all sitting around the supper table, I said, "Your goddamn boy hung my mule." Tiny Fran almost swallowed her tongue. I told her to shut up before she said anything, and then I said, "You heard me. Your boy hung my mule, and I want to know where he is so I can kill the sonofabitch." I went on and told them I knew it was him on account of how I'd walked up on him and two of the Snipes boys teasing Sugar Pete about a week before, talking about how stupid she looked, poking at her, and how I told them I'd get my pistol out if they didn't get on back down the road. Tiny Fran wanted to try to say something again and Burr told her just to stay out of it, that it was I and his business.

Then Burr got up from the table and said to go with him back to the living room and we'd talk about it. Then he told me he felt like the whole thing was part-way his fault for how he'd sent Roland over to my house to feed up in his place that Saturday evening. They'd called a grange meeting he had to go to. And then he said it wasn't a doubt in his mind that Roland was the ringleader, that it was pure evil and had his name all over it. I know Burr felt real bad. He said he'd try and make it right.

We went on back in the kitchen and Tiny Fran was slamming dishes in the sink, and Burr went over to the china closet and got me a hundred-dollar bill out of a little pitcher. He told me to take it and buy Ruby another mule. He even said he'd take me to the stockyard on sale day to help me find a good one. But before that bill hit my hand Tiny Fran swung around from the sink and yelled out, "I was saving that money for a dishwasher!" Burr just went on and put the money in my hand, and listen to me, he said, "Woman, you've got two perfectly good dishwashers, the right hand and the left one." She said a few choice words and headed out the door. I had to laugh although I hated to in the middle of this about Sugar Pete. June got up from the table and said she was going to see Ruby, and Burr said to go on and see her.

I look back on it now and feature myself slamming Tiny Fran back in a chair just like she was slamming those dishes, and I tell her, "Listen here, you knew when you had him he was a goddamn monster. You bound to! A mama ought to know! If I was you I'd have been punching him in the goddamn mouth everytime he opened it to speak the past sixteen years. Leastways he shouldn't have been out, mean as he is, out around in somebody's business. If I had a rattlesnake I'd keep him locked up in a glass box where folks can tap and tap all they want to and not have to worry about getting bit, same thing with your little bastard."

I bought another mule with Burr's money. We called him Sugar Pete after the first one. He had a strong back and a nice curve to him and eyes Ruby said looked full of sense. When we unloaded him out of the trailer I led him up under the kitchen window just like I'd led the first Sugar Pete and I hollered, "Ruby!" And she came to the window and looked and then came on out the door, taking off her apron and saying, "Look at this!" I put her up on him and led her up and down the path a time or two. He was real easy to just have been bought. We had a good time with him, but to tell the truth, you couldn't hardly look at him and not think of the first Sugar Pete. And after Ruby died I couldn't hardly bear to look at him. I sold him to a boy up the road here. You hate to do it but you have to.

Leastways neither I don't have to look at Roland. I hope they threw away the damn key. I know Stella Morgan wasn't a Ivory Girl, but she didn't deserve what he did to her. People won't say much about it, never did, but I guarantee if it'd been a black boy that did it the KKK and the Rights of White People nuts would've been out here marching and raising all grades of hell up and down the highway. It's not that Burr tried to cover it up or protect Roland from it being publicized. He wouldn't even pay for him a lawyer. One of Tiny Fran's gripes was that if they'd got him somebody down here from New York City he'd have gone free. I wanted to tell her, "Bullshit. Perry Mason working Della Street and Paul Drake overtime couldn't have defended that boy." And the stupidest part of it all was he raped Stella Morgan while he was on probation for something he'd done almost as disgusting.

Listen and tell me if you don't hear something that won't turn your stomach. Roland was eighteen years old, about to get out of school, and Burr sent him to the FCX to get something and instead of going and doing what he was supposed to do he went and did something else. He went in the nice new big department store downtown and got a pair of scissors and had himself a little party, cut the crotches out from between the legs of some nice ladies' drawers.

Burr was in a state of shock when the sheriff called and said what he had Roland locked up for. I was ashamed to tell Ruby. Then all they did was make him see a doctor, and then the doctor said Roland wasn't so messed up he couldn't live amongst the rest of us, so they put him on probation and told him to do so many hours of community service.

You want to hear Roland's idea of serving the community? He got a date with Stella when she was living at Ruth's, and he got her shut up in Burr's car and near about beat the life out of her. Ellen, one of the girls that stayed up at Ruth's with her, told Ruby how late one night they heard something sounded like all hell breaking loose in front of the house, then a car door slamming, then tires squalling, and Ellen said she got to the front door and looked out and saw Burr's car tearing up down the highway. She said she thought, Where's Stella? Then she thought, That sorry Roland Stanley. She said she could see Stella, looking like something off a monster movie with that full moon hitting her beat-up face, trying to pull herself up off the ditchbank. Her and Ruth took her to town, and soon as they got her checked in the emergency room she got hold of the sheriff and told about seeing Burr's taillights.

And to top the whole thing off, he went and did the one thing it couldn't anybody forgive him for, if you could ever excuse him for Stella. He left her there at Ruth's and went right on home and went to bed. He didn't even wipe the blood off the car seat, didn't even lock himself up in his room. No, he just crawled in the bed and covered his head, wearing his pajamas, like he was daring somebody to come in and accuse him, like he was a goddamn Boy Scout or something. I think if he'd have run just a little ways people wouldn't despise him as much as they do. See, him playing big man with the law was too big a insult to people out here. He ought to've run some. But he let the sheriff walk right in his room and get him, won't no chasing or catching to it, and Tiny Fran standing in the yard boo-hooing the whole damn time.

She tried her best to spread the blame for what became of him deep and wide, her standing in the middle of it all pronouncing judgment on everybody but herself. I and Ruby always knew she was thinking if she let him do anything he pleased then he'd grow up right, grow up and give her more attention than her daddy did and Burr did and anybody else did that had to associate with her. I used to see the boy come home from elementary school, get his milk bottle off the table and pour him a big old bottle full of chocolate milk and lay down in front of the cartoons and suck on it until suppertime. Burr told me for every milk bottle he threw in the trash Tiny Fran'd bring two more in the house. He said he finally told her he was washing his hands of it.

Even after all was said and done and Roland was locked up, she still went around saying modern society had to take some of the blame for what happened to him. Burr said she'd picked that talk up from Roland's lawyer, and he thought about as much of it as I did. I told him, I said, "Roland wasn't part of society to begin with." I went on and said, "Unless society came out past Flat Rock Crossroads, kept on past Booker T. High School, hung two rights, a left, turned in on Milk Farm Road and found Roland plowing a tobacco field, jerked him off the tractor, warped him and set him back up there without anybody riding by and noticing, blame can't be laid on society." And I told Burr too I think folks in town in general try to think too goddamn much.

Why couldn't have somebody just as easily said he was mean, mean to the core, and then drove pure crazy with his mama all the time twisting what he was needing up with what she was needing, and then something clicked in that car and he let what was stove up come flying out? And as for what was on his mind when it clicked, I'd put my last dollar on it being Tiny Fran. You don't have to be a smart town somebody to figure that out.

12.

When it rains it pours! Sometimes things happen and they pile up on you so fast you don't know if you'll ever settle back down, catch up again. All yesterday, all day yesterday all I did was think, and then I waited for Jack, waited for him twice to come home and spell me from all my thoughts. Then when he came in and we rested and ate it seemed like the whole long day started over. I had to wind back up again. I stay tired enough now as it is.

Somebody knocked on the front door about eight. Nobody ever comes to the front besides encyclopedia salesmen, Jehovah's Witnesses, or lay witness missionaries from down at Ephesus Free Will Baptist, and I thought to myself, Which one is it tonight and how can we get rid of him? And we couldn't pretend to be gone, not with all the lights on and Jack's game show blaring. He got up and peeked out of the front window and I had my fingers crossed for the salesman or the Jehovah's Witnesses because they pretty much have to believe Jack when he says we just bought a whole set or just joined the church down the road, but the lay witness people know my husband has never warmed a pew at Ephesus Free Will, and neither have I. But Jack closed the curtain and said, "Hot damn, Ruby. It's Cecil Spangler and he's got his Bible with him." I told him to have fun and that I'd be at the kitchen table cutting out June's skirt, but he wasn't listening to me. He was too busy thinking up what sort of game he wanted to play with Cecil.

See, Jack had rather worry and agitate Cecil Spangler than eat when he's hungry. Whenever he sees him at the store or the stockyard or somewhere he always comes back home and runs back through how he chased Cecil round and round on some religious issue, like the virgin birth or the seven-day creation, and how Cecil wound up on the short end, embarrassed in front of a whole gang of men, them no doubt egging Jack on. And as many times as Jack's come in the door saying, "I ran into old Saint Cecil today," you'd think he would hide when he sees Jack coming, but there he was at our door last night, asking for it. Sometimes you have to wonder if he doesn't enjoy being persecuted, thrive on it.

Cecil's one of those people who're constantly preoccupied with the church, sin in the world, their souls and everybody else's. He's even told people around here that his goal is to live like Jesus, walk where he walked. I remember one Saturday morning I was up at the store with Jack, he and the boys were showing me how to work the pinball game, and Cecil came right up to us and said Jesus would never have played any betting games or wasted hard-earned money on devilish amusement. Jack let his ball roll right through the little trap and he turned around and told Cecil, "Yeah, and I bet you Jesus didn't have a satellite dish in his yard half the size of yours. And you owe me a quarter for that game, oh ye of all that faith." Everybody in the store hooted. I wanted to tell Cecil he'd had it coming to him, but I suppose he knew, just like last night.

And last night wouldn't have been different from any of those other times if Cecil had just not mentioned my illness. But he did, and what used to be a way for Jack to show off how sharp and quick he is turned mean and malicious, and my husband is not a mean man. Last night drained him. I hope it's nothing we'll ever again go through. Maybe the next time Cecil gets the urge to pray over poor old Ruby he'll do it from a distance. He'd be crazy to come here and try it again.

While I'm on all this, I know how it would make perfectly good sense for me to reach out to religion now. People prepare to meet their maker every day. You think of all the war movies with the priest going around in the infirmary, doing the last rites for the soldiers, all the forgiving and being forgiven. But see, my problem with all that is I don't believe I had a maker. I don't believe anybody did, not Jack, not even Cecil Spangler. It's just not the way Jack and I think things are organized, if you can call everything that goes on organization. We'd just rather stay amazed at how it all happens, I mean this world bumping right along with no plan at all. I'm not exactly sure where I've gotten everything I think about this, certainly not from the way I was raised. I guess I've just been making things up along the way and accumulating what did me good, throwing out ideas that didn't, and I bet you that's not a far cry from the way this world works.

Thinking about dying, I'm not half as worried or depressed over it as I bet Cecil would be if he were in my shoes, thinking he's bound to be headed one way and then having that doubt come in, you know it's bound to, and nip at all that confidence. What I mostly feel is a sadness over knowing I won't ever be physically here again, here in my house, at my table, with Jack. But Cecil and I do see eye-to-eye on one thing, leaving here is nowhere near the end.

See, I believe that when I die my spirit and my body,

tired and worn out as it'll be, will separate, slip apart, and my spirit will live and see all and know all it couldn't before, and it won't matter what becomes of the body. The spirit can and will go and do as it can and will. I get more comfort out of believing my parents and grandparents are with me that way, rather than that they're somewhere I can't get to until I'm dead, when I won't need to feel them the way I've needed to lately.

Jack believes this too, and he says it like this, that the soul will come aloose and fly off and "do anything it damn well pleases." He says, like I do, that the body was made to give out. We talked about all that before we were married, times I'd cook supper for him and we'd sit out on the steps in the night air. And we kept on talking about our living and dying until I got sick. I guess it was easier for Jack to face the idea of dying when the real thing wasn't living in the same house with him.

But back on last night. Cecil came in, settled in, and I heard him say, "Where's the wife?" I had a mouthful of pins, and before I could get them out, Jack answered for me. I stuck my head out of the kitchen door and waved at him.

Then Jack asked Cecil what sort of burden he had weighing on his heart. He said, "Seems like you've always got some burden or other weighing on you. Just spit it out."

Cecil said, "Well, I do. I've come here tonight with a

heavy, heavy heart. You see, we down at Ephesus know what a terrible time you and Ruby must be going through, her finding out what she did and all, and the preacher and the whole membership just wanted me to come down here tonight and try once again to extend the right hand of Christian fellowship and let you know that it's never too late to accept the Lord Jesus Christ as your personal savior." He got every last bit of that out and I don't believe I heard him take a breath. And at first what he said about me finding out what I did didn't hit me, but then I realized he was talking about the cancer, and I could almost feel something shooting straight through me.

I listened for Jack to come back at that, but he was quiet, I know planning exactly how much rope he intended to give Cecil. Then he said, "Oh, you did, did you? Well then why don't you just go right ahead. See, you've got to kind of sweeten the pot a little bit if you expect me to let my wife to jump in it." You could hear the sarcasm in it, at least I did, but Cecil was too pleased and too eager to hear anything other than that this heathen couple might finally be ready to be won. Maybe a better woman than me would've gotten up and gone in there and found a way to get Cecil out of the house, but whatever it was that'd struck me when he mentioned my illness had me bolted down. I just could not find it in me to stop what I knew was coming.

Didn't Cecil think this was a little odd? I guess not. He just said he'd be more than willing to share the good news, and he started with the "In my Father's house there are many mansions" psalm. I thought, Of all the poems in that Bible, surely you could've found a less depressing one. But when he'd finished Jack said, "You read real good!" Then I thought, Well, Ruby, at least you can laugh.

Cecil thanked Jack, not offended at all, and then proceeded to explain the verse, going all into the streets of silver and gold, eternal jubilation and so forth. Then he said, "Yes, and 'I've got a mansion just over the hilltop, in that bright land where we'll never grow old,' and if you and your wife just say the word you can have that too." I couldn't help but think of all those shows Jack has watched about no-money-down real estate. All Jack said was, "That sounds just too good to be true!" I had to get those pins out of my mouth before I swallowed one laughing.

Then Cecil said the damned had an awful destiny, none of the specially prepared mansions and what-not. And Jack told him he'd like to hear all he had on hell, seeing as how he'd been told to go there so much. I didn't hear Cecil laugh. Either he didn't think it was funny or he was so caught up in what he was saying that he didn't catch it. But Jack went on to say he thought hell always sounded a mite bit trumped up, all the red devils, fire and brimstone and so forth, and he wanted Cecil to straighten everything out for him. I'd never heard anything like it. But he jumped right in Jack's trap and told him, "Hell? It's worse than anything you could ever imagine. There's no place like hell." I couldn't help but see that old devil clicking those cloven hooves. And then Cecil went on and on about all the screaming agony, suckling babies being torn from their mothers, all that torture and it thousands and thousands of degrees and all of it lasting forever. Then Jack asked him if they might would let him stoke a furnace. I had to stop cutting out again and laugh out loud. But Cecil didn't hear me. He didn't seem to have heard Jack. And the saddest part of all this was knowing he was actually believing everything he was saying just as if he'd been there and was now back to tell about it. It was like Jack was asking Cecil to recommend somewhere for us to go on vacation and Cecil was explaining all the reasons we ought to pick somewhere like Disneyland over New York City.

Then Jack told him he wanted more detail, and I thought to myself, Cecil is absolutely too deep into this to dig himself out and it's going to take Jack and a stick of dynamite to blow him up out of that hell he's created. And that's what it took. But first Cecil went on and gave Jack all the extra details he wanted, even down to whores and whoremongers grinding and sliding all over each other, men with men and women with women, sordid and repulsive, and all of it very unnatural. Then I heard Jack yell out, "I know it! I read all about it!" And Cecil told him he was glad he'd struck a chord, how everything he'd been talking about was all there in black and white in the greatest book ever written. He said he was glad something from that book had stuck with him. Then Jack was about screaming trying to get Cecil to tune in and listen hard. He yelled out, "Yes, all this has done rung a bell! And you're not lying about it being the good book. We about wore it out at the store looking at it, cover came off." He kept on and on about how much he enjoyed it and how glad he was that Cecil had read the same thing, and then he told him he'd been under the impression that the story had taken place in Paris, France, not hell. And he said, "That fellow did the ungodliest things with a whole roomful of folks!"

I couldn't stand just listening, not seeing this, so I got up and stood in the kitchen door. Neither one of them noticed me. Poor Cecil was about to explode. He whacked that Bible on his leg and yelled out, "You cannot blaspheme the Holy Word! You cannot make a mockery of God's Word!" Jack played dumb and told him, "Well, I was just trying to show you how you're not the only one with good reading tastes."

Then Cecil said, "All I came here to do tonight was to show you how the Word might lead you, save you from your sins." He said God's Word was the message of salvation and he thought that might offer us some hope in these last hours. I was absolutely appalled.

Jack changed. All that sarcasm came right to the surface and he said, "I'll tell you something. They say the meek will inherit the earth, but I think you and the whole Free Wheeling Baptist bunch of you will be caught a day late and a dollar short because a meek man wouldn't have the gall it took to come down here tonight knowing about Ruby, and that's none of your business anyway. And I'll tell you another thing. I know the word, and the word is leave, get the hell out of my house before I get my pistol out."

Cecil'd seen me in the door by then. It looked like the same thing that'd shot through me earlier was now going through him, and he said, "Ruby, I'm sorry as I can be if anybody misunderstood me."

I told him it was between Jack and him, but I did think the best thing to do would be for him to leave right then. And then Jack hopped right in and said, "Misunderstood? Misundertook is more like it. Now get the hell out of my house." And Cecil did. He left without another word.

Jack looked like he'd lost the war, not won it, shaky, red-faced. I told him to come in the kitchen and I'd fix him a bowl of ice cream or something, but he said he had something to take care of outside first. I knew where he was going, and it's so seldom he takes a drink with me sick that I just let him go.

He came on back in when I was about asleep, and he crawled in the bed beside me, all his clothes still on. I know he was afraid he'd fall down undressing in the dark. I backed up into him and let him hold me, and I could smell his breath just as sweet and thick as it could be. Then he kissed my hair and said, " 'Night, 'night, Ruby. See you in the morning."

Oh, Cecil and all his heaven talk, he just doesn't know. I have what I need back there stirring now, about to call out any second and ask me if I saved him any coffee.

13.

I'm finally at the point, past the point, where I can say this and mean it and not have to worry over somebody saying to eat my hat. I'm sick of being by myself, sick of myself, sick all the way around of looking around and not seeing a damn thing but the four walls and my old ugly self looking back out of dirty, smeared up mirrors. Ruby'd be ashamed. This place looks like the pigs slept in it, and I walk around all day looking like the witches rode me all night, raggedy, messy. I know it but I haven't been able to do anything about it. You just can't expect a man to take and do without a woman when he's done with one long as I did.

Be two weeks ago tomorrow I finished all Ruby's food. I looked down in that deep freeze all raw cold and empty and said, What're you going to do now? I told Burr about it and he told me, he said, "I told you you ought to've let me help you get some bean rows in, least a hill or two." Then he told me I could walk across the field and take a meal with him whenever I wanted to, but I turned him down. I want to eat in my own damn house.

So I started out on cornflakes, and when I got sick of cornflakes I opened a can of soup, damn old watery-tasting soup. It won't long before I said, Not only are you going to rot here, you're going to starve too! I'd been used to a big meal. Cornflakes and soup won't hold a man. I know how to cook, the getting-by kind of cooking a man'll do, but that don't mean I want to do it. And I cooked what Ruby'd froze according to how I thought I was supposed to, but that don't mean it was always fit to eat. What I mean to say is, I was hungry for something good!

Then I thought of something. I said, Isn't it some cooking shows Ruby used to sit here and watch off the public television? I found one in the afternoon, sat here with a pencil and paper like she would, and I watched and wrote, watched and wrote. Sounded good, garlicky chicken in some lemon juice. I must've been a idiot to think I could have something like that, but I went on to the store anyway.

Porter had some nice fresh chicken in, a lemon too, but that was about all he had except for my regular groceries. If you can't boil it, fry it, or scoop it out of the can then he generally won't stock it. But I got to thinking about that garlic, how I like a good strong taste, and I said, Well, you won't know if he has some hid somewhere if you don't ask him, so I did. And did I evermore get hooted and hollered at. One somebody asked me if I was planning to hang some around my neck to keep the vampires off me. I and the boys have always been real tight but I told them every last one to go to hell and I meant it. I took my grocery bag and left.

What was I thinking to think a store that keeps bloodworms in the cooler with the chicken and cube steaks might stock something good as garlic? Then all I could taste was Ruby's spaghetti sauce, and I wanted to take and pitch that damn chicken out in the highway. And it didn't come out right either, right red raw in the middle, but I ate it anyway.

Come along about Thursday I said, It's bound to be more than one way to skin this cat. Ruby used to say you just always had to believe you'd find as many answers as it was questions, and I had three big questions every day I needed a answer to, What's for breakfast? What's for lunch? What's for supper? To hell with the snacks. Then I was talking to Burr and he said, "What you need is to get you somebody in there to help you out." I told him he might be right, I could get used to having somebody to wait on me. When Ruby got so sick her sister-in-law came down here and stayed a month with us, wouldn't let neither I nor Ruby one touch a dirty dish, but Ruby tried, kept trying until she couldn't try no more. But I said I bet Jimmy wouldn't let go of Elsie to come and stay with me by myself, and Burr told me he had something in mind. I said, "Well, what?" And he just said, "Come on get in the truck and let's take a ride." So I did.

He said he was taking me out to the old Butler place, said it might still be one or two working-age women left out there who wouldn't mind picking up a dollar or two. He said most of the tenants that farmed for the old lady Butler had about all moved to town when the old lady died and they brought in all the big machinery and what-not but he'd heard a few hung on out there. I said, "I know how it is, you stay somewhere so long and you feel like you want to leave and then somebody says you can leave and then you don't feel like you can." I could've left Henry Hoover when daddy died, found something to do in town, but I said, No, I 'bout as well stay.

But anyway, we rode on out there and I and Burr both looked at the homeplace and just had to shake our head. You ought to listen a minute about the Butler crowd because they're really something to talk about. They're most of them dead, except for the ones in town and the grand-daughter and her husband that live on the place now and do a half-assed job farming it. The girl's some kin to June's friend Ellen, but you couldn't hold a gun to her and get her to claim them.

You ought to've seen what the Butler lady did to me one time. Used to I used to like to ride Ruby's bicycle up and down the highway and pick up drink bottles, that was before everything was in a can. I'd ride all over hell and half of Georgia, and some days I'd start on home with that basket filled up so full that all that bicycle acted like it wanted to do was turn over. But I liked doing it. Found money. You can't turn your nose up at found money. And anyway, one morning early I was riding along and I saw this big cream-colored car coming right towards me, and it kept coming and coming, and then it sort of eased over to my side of the road, and right before I turned into the ditch I saw that mean little woman all hunched up behind the steering wheel laughing like a hyena! I was afraid she might stop and get out and shoot me laying there with Ruby's bicycle on top of me, but she just went on down the road. It shook me up fairly bad, and you can damn well better bet I stayed off that stretch of road until I heard that woman was dead in the ground.

Before she died though that place was something to see, big, big old white house. I remember riding by there on the way to the tobacco market one time, sitting in back in case the tarp wanted to fly off, and I remember seeing her out in front of the house standing over a colored man while he painted the birdbath. I just had to wonder what it'd be like if I'd been born a rich somebody with money.

But it's not so fine a place now, weeds up in the yard high as my hip, and that birdbath busted, laying on the ground, the whole business just gone to pure ruination, ruination time'll do if you let it. Burr told me when we were out there, he said one time he had to go see the old lady about some hay and he got up in the yard and damned if she didn't have a whole row of colored women lined up all the way down one side of the house cleaning the windows, one woman on a window, inside and out.

And I bet you not a window on that house has been touched since she died. I told Burr, I said, "Mine's about that filthy," and he told me just to hang on, he'd find me some help. He said if it didn't work out he'd send June back to my house this weekend to give it a good going-through. I said I hated to ask June to have to come back in and mess in my mess, but you get in this shape and you can't be too choicey.

Anyway, I and Burr drove all back through the old lady's yard, all past the equipment shelters, past the irrigation pond, about dried up, and then coming around the curve I saw a big dried out field full of houses, old people, old cars. This is exactly what it was like, it was like somebody'd took a notion to decorate the place and said, "Here, here's some houses" and pitched some little shacks out over the field. Then he said, "Here, have some people" and threw out a handful or two of people the way you sling corn over chickens.

We pulled up in front of one of the houses and the screen door opened and the biggest, coal-blackest woman I'd ever seen stepped out. She came right over to my side of the truck, walking without bending her knees, more waddling than walking. Burr told me her name was Mavis Washington and she'd helped him barn tobacco a few times. He said she was a card.

Then listen. She said, "How you doing, Mr. Stanley? Who ya'll looking fo'?" Burr told her I was looking for some housekeeping help, and did she know anybody who wanted to work.

She laughed and fanned herself with both her hands and she said, "It ain't nobody likes to but we all does it." Then she reached in her bosom, listen now, right in front of two white men she reached down in her bosom and started pulling out this white rag, something looking like a baby diaper, and she kept on pulling like it was a magic trick. Then when it was all out she wiped her face and neck all around and ran the rag up one arm. I thought, Good God.

While she was swabbing herself Burr said, "Well, what do you think? Think you might could help us?"

Then she crammed that rag back down there and without even looking up from her business she said, "What do it pay?"

I told her ten dollars a day, three days a week, a Monday, Wednesday and Friday, plus all the meals.

Then she leaned her head back the way they do when they have the spirit and she said, "Lawd, if ya'll ain't something!" Then she laughed. Then she said, "I reckon if I fixin' to cook I fixin' to eat it too!"

Burr laughed but I wondered what to do. See, when he asked if she might could help us, I thought she'd take it like, "Can you help us find somebody besides yourself?" But she took it the opposite and hired herself before I could think straight. A big woman pulling out of her bosom'll throw you off.

Then I thought to myself, I bet that woman can make biscuits the kind you dream of. So I went on and told her she could start work soon as she was able, next day if she could. She asked me if I'd carry her back and forth or should her boys. I told her her boys.

Burr cranked the truck and I said for her to be there first thing bright and early to see how I had things set up and what-not. And then she started cramming her rag back down in that bosom and asking me how to get to my house. I told her how to look for it across Burr's field and said it was a silver mailbox in front with Jack Stokes on it.

She just took off yelling, "Whew! You Blinking Jack?" I told her I was and she said, "Lawd, Lawd. Them days I was up to Mr. Stanley's barn all I be hearing was, 'Blinking Jack he say this, Blinking Jack he done that. Shame he ain't here, always cutting up, being funny,' and I say, 'Where he is?' and they say, 'To the hills with his wife.' I say, 'Well, I sho' would likes to meet somebody loves to laugh and carry on foolishness. Mavis do love to laugh.' " That kind of got away with me, then I thought to myself, Well, Mavis loves to laugh, I sure as hell hope Mavis loves to work.

So she got there the next morning, not early, I'd already had my cereal. I stood there at the front door and waited for her and I looked around my house and thought, I have a mess, a good woman comes to clean wants a mess, must crave a man's mess. I held open the door and in she comes up the steps not bending those knees, like she's wood. She grabbed the door and said, "My knees is killing me. It must be 'gwine rain." She went on in and put this big old satchel down on the kitchen table and proceeded to take out all grades of mess and lay it all out over the table. She said, "I likes to be able to gets to my bidnis." I stood watching her, wondering if I ought to've let her come here. Something was way, way off.

Then here comes her business out of the bag. It was first a sack of hard Christmas candy, then orange jelly slices. She looked at me, slid both of them across the table and said to me, "I likes to have something sweets to suck on. You welcome to it." I told her no thank you, and then she took out two all stretched-out-looking Ace bandages, lotion, two snuff cans, a white Bible, a big wad of rags like I told about, two tall grape drinks, and a round donut pillow. About that last thing, she laid it on the table and said, "This is for when I sits."

I stood there fairly well amazed. Then she picked up her old stretched-out bandages and said, "I gots to wrap these knees fo' I starts to pulling and stooping. They all swoll up." Her legs! Whew! Looked like they'd pure blow up if you put a pin to them, big around as my whole head. I told her to go on back to the bathroom, and she went on back and directly I heard something sounded like the whole toilet stool was tearing off the wall. I took and went back there and got by the door and hollered, "What are you doing? Be careful with my toilet stool!" She said she was just doing her business and to go on.

She finally came out but she still had the bandages in her hand. She said to me, "You got a wobbly toilet. I can't wrap on no wobbly toilet." I told her it didn't wobble ten minutes ago. Then she just said again, "You got you a wobbly toilet," and she proceeded to sit down in Ruby's chair. I could just see the whole thing buckle. Look what she did to the toilet! So I told her to find somewhere else to park it. She went over to my big old stuffed chair I sit and watch the television in. It's real low to the floor, and before she was halfway down I said, "You get down, you won't get back up." Last thing a man needs is a big woman stuck in his television chair. So she looked around for somewhere she could sit and not break or get swallowed in and I wanted to say, "It must be a whole lot of trouble being as large as you, can't even sit down regular." Then she spotted Ruby's kitchen stool with the back to it and she said, "That looks just right." Right soon as she said that I hung a pair of yellow pigtails on her and featured her like a big old black Goldilocks. It looked real odd to me.

It was nigh about noon when she finally got her knees fixed and all that mess on the table in order. I figured I'd leave for awhile. I figured she might not want to clean with me in the house. Ruby used to take the broom and act like she was sweeping me out the door. So I went on and helped Burr fix his transmission and then I went on back. I walked in the kitchen and said to myself, Lord God! Everything was just like I'd left it, dishes strung out hither to yon, grease and mess caked on the stove. And you want to know where Mavis was? She was sitting on the couch with her head slung all back, like if I didn't think she was alive I'd have thought she was dead, holding onto the broom like she was paddling a boat. I poked her on the arm and told her to wake up. She liked to've jumped fifty feet. Then she rubbed her eyes and told me, she said, "I went to sweeping and my knees just give out on me, sleeping when I suppose to be sweeping." Then she laughed and laughed, wiping her eyes, and she told me, "Whew! Mavis do love to laugh! I finish it the next time." I thought, What? I told her if she was so sore she shouldn't have hired herself out, and she ought to look around, that she wouldn't see any signs up saying I hire the handicapped. She just said my mouth was as bad as she'd heard it was, and then she laughed some more and got herself up off the couch.

As soon as she put Ruby's broom up she looked at the kitchen clock and said, "Whew Lawd! I needs to call Nathan to get me." And I thought, Oh shit. Then she asked me, she said, "Where's the telefoam?" I told her I didn't have one, I'd let it go a few months ago, and the closest one was Burr's house right across the field. I pointed out the window. She said, "My knees is already give out. I can't do no walking." I thought to myself, I bet if the nearest telephone was at the honey bun factory you'd run over me getting out the door. But I didn't feel like getting her started back up. I just wanted her to go home, so I went on to Burr's and used his phone and said for Nathan to come carry his mama home.

The next time she got here about the same time, late, and strowed all her mess out over the table again. I told her, I said, "Mavis, I've got to go to help Burr out over yonder and when I get back I expect to see something done, like the dishes washed, the floors swept, and so forth and so on." And I said for her to watch herself with the toilet stool. She won't half listening to me, bent way over, sticking her grape drinks in the refrigerator. She just said, "Somebody needs to do something about this nasty icebox." I just thought, Lord God, and I wonder who.

Burr liked to've laughed his head off when I told him all about Mavis. I said, "You pay somebody ten dollars to cook and clean and then you eat chicken noodle soup out of the last clean bowl, you pay somebody all that money and see how hard you laugh." He said he didn't mean to laugh but it was still funny.

That afternoon I went on back across the field and I got closer and closer and I saw some clothes on the line, then I got closer and saw it was my work shirts and dungarees, then I got right near up on the yard and said, "What's it doing with spots on them?" She'd bleached my clothes! I wanted to jerk a knot in her. I went in the door and yelled at her, I said, "What's it doing with spots on my dungarees? You don't bleach dungarees!" And listen to what she said to me, she said, "I got mixed up." I said, "What?" And she just said, "I got mixed up I'm telling you," and then she started back on what she was doing, which was opening one of her grape drinks between her knees. I thought to myself, Those knees won't hold you to mop but they'll hold a grape drink. Then she took her drink in the living room and eased down on her donut pillow and started shaking her head. I followed her in there and asked her what was going on, and she said to me, "I sho' wish you had a telefoam." All I could say was for her to give me the damn number again, and I went on and called her boy. I told Burr about it and when he got through laughing he said he'd send June out here next weekend.

Nathan came and got her and I told her it wasn't any need for her to come anymore, and I gave her twenty dollars plus five more for gas her boy used hauling her. I went on back in the house and said, "Well, I wipe my hands of that," and I took and got a wrench and fixed my toilet.

See, it had sounded like the perfect setup to me. Didn't it you? Isn't it every man's dream that when his wife dies he has somebody to step in and do for him? I guess Ruby was right on the mark when she used to catch me sending off for something about how to make a million dollars and say to me, "If something sounds too good to be true, it usually is. Give me the envelope. Save that stamp to mail a bill with." I listened to her then. I'd listen to her now. I just wish it was somebody here like her now that could tell me what to do.

14.

Jack hasn't had much to say today. I've sewn all day.

A little while ago he came and stood beside me with his hands in his pockets and asked me what I was doing. I said, "Well, Jack, I'm sewing." He's so preoccupied with last night. I told him he should walk over to Burr's, that I didn't need him for anything until supper, but he won't leave here today. I also told him we could go sit outside when I finished this skirt. It's warm for November.

I told June I'd have her things ready by Saturday. I hope everything fits, hangs right. I'd hate for her to go off on her trip looking homemade. Nothing looks worse.

Jack can't think of a thing to do, so the television goes on. Maybe he'll fall asleep in front of it. He needs to either be distracted or asleep. Last night's just eating at him.

Suppose he hadn't been here? Would Cecil have talked

to me by myself? I don't think so. I've always believed that Cecil and most everybody out here are a little afraid of me. They always seem to speak to me through Jack, like, "Jack, how'd you and Ruby like your trip to the mountains?" and I'm standing right there. They think it's odd, I know they do, they think it's peculiar as it can be, me married to him. Nobody's understood, or tried to, except Burr and June and my family. I used to feel the urge to justify us to everybody who stared, but then it passed. Even the urge to tell women at the store that it was none of their business, that passed too. Maybe I just got used to being stared at. That's people. You can't change them for the world. One time, when we were first married, I told Jack how it bothered me, all the looking and knowing I was being talked about at every supper table up and down Milk Farm Road, and he said, "If they can't find one thing to talk about, they'll find another." And that comes from a man who's lived on this road all his life, been talked about at all those supper tables, if not for his blinking then for his weight, and if not for that then for being an old tenant married to somebody twenty years younger.

Mama and daddy were the only people I felt like I needed to explain anything to, and I finally did, but before I got to talking about Jack I had so many other things to cover. They sat and listened, so did Sudie Bee. Jack was out looking at the farm with Paul and Jimmy. We'd agreed that I should talk to mama and daddy by myself awhile. When I finished, mama said, "Well, I guess you've about done it all!" Who'd have thought you could do it all without leaving the South? And then later that day I heard Sudie Bee in the pantry with Lester, filling him in on everything I'd said, and she told him, "Shame the law don't allow Miss Ruby to marry her daddy. All she be wanting is to marry her daddy."

I did want somebody to take care of me. I needed it. And when I felt all that goodness coming from Jack, it didn't matter what the person looked like that sent it out to me. Maybe I did want a daddy, but that's okay, too. I never heard any bells ringing and so forth, but look what'd happened to me when I did! The quiet kind of love is better than the other, lasted longer, been better to us. Oh, it's no crime to want and need somebody to love and to be loved by and to go and do what you need to do to have that, but it's certainly a pity when you want it so badly you'll let it be anybody.

And I certainly went from good to bad to good mighty quick. And now the bad's coming again, and it'll get worse and worse, and Jack'll have to be here with me and see me, and he'll have to say, "Look what's become of this woman I married." If I'd knelt down with Cecil maybe I'd be looking forward to good again, but I couldn't do that. I'll just wish and try to make it so for Jack. My brothers have promised to check on him, and I made Burr promise me the day after I was diagnosed to do anything he could here, June, too. And when I've finished this skirt for her I'll go out to the freezer and look at everything and try to feel better. I'm counting on that working. And then I'll come back in and see if Jack's ready to go outside with me, and we'll sit out there together until it's too late to see the pine trees across the field.

15.

I washed my sheets for the first time in two months this morning, first time since June was here and stripped the bed down. They're white, needed some bleach, but it won't a drop left on account of Mavis going wild with it. I'm going to dye my dungarees back blue.

Know why I took and washed my sheets this morning? I did it for Ruby. It was Ruby that told me to do it. In a way it was Ruby.

See, last night I was laid in bed sleeping, just sleeping regular, and then I went to roll over and I couldn't. What it was like was like it was somebody laying next to me on top of the covers. I thought it might be one of the dogs got in the house and crawled up in with me, but then I said it'd take Lassie to undo a lock and get in here. I went to turn again and I still couldn't. Then I thought I might've been just mixed up the first time. You know how it is when you wake up like that and think you're doing something like getting some water and then you don't know if you did or you didn't.

Then I said, This is how Ruby used to do, how she used to lay on top of the covers when she'd get hot in the night. I'd have to wake her up and tell her I couldn't sleep with her weighting the sheet down, keeping me from turning. And last night when I felt that same feeling I was pure scared to turn my head around and check her spot. Can't you imagine!

I laid there still as I could and next thing I knew I was asleep again. First thing I did this morning was I got up and looked at her spot real close, looking for a dent like a body'd leave. I didn't see one, but I said, That don't mean she won't here! Then I said, A spirit don't have weight. But if it was Ruby and she wanted to be here with me awhile, she could take weight. She could do anything she wants to! Nothing stopping her!

See, every night I've laid in bed and wished Ruby was over there sleeping, laying on top of the covers, reading with the lights on, sitting up eating yogurt, just everything she used to do. I've wished so hard you could call it begging. And I thought, Of all the things I've wished for and I've not got, I've finally come through with this one.

But don't run out and start wishing. It's all got to be just right, like ripe for you. Nine and three-quarters times out of ten wishing won't make a thing so, but you hit it one time and you'll run around like somebody with no sense, like I have today. Not every man can wish a dead wife back. Suppose you bad-mouthed your wife, pulled mean drunks and beat her, and then she dies one day. Then you sit around saying how bad you wish you could make it up to her. Do you think she'd show up and give you another chance after the way she was pushed and pulled the first go-round? She'd be a fool to. And you'd be a bigger fool wasting time wishing. She'd just stay off somewhere and let you suffer.

I and Ruby watched all the Topper movies. We used to joke about hainting all the time. And last night I bet she was missing me like I was missing her, missing her all the nights she'd scramble around in and out of the covers, and I'd say, "Ruby, how about decide if you're hot or cold," and she'd go to sleep with one leg in and one leg out because she said she couldn't make up her mind.

But I was just real touched by her coming, and what I have planned to do is to woo her into coming tonight. I know you can't catch a haint and hold it forever, but don't you know I would if I could? Don't you know some you would?

Before I put the clean sheets back on I plan to sprinkle some of Ruby's smelly-good powders over the mattress, shake some down in the pillow case. All her woman stuff's still on her bureau. I haven't moved anything. I don't know what I'd do with any of it. And it's not mine to be giving away or throwing out. I'd rather let Burr come in here after I'm gone and decide what'll become of our business. But I'll fix her room up for her. I figure why would a woman, be she dead or otherwise, want to crawl in a musty bed with the sheets gray? I'm tempted to lay down with my two-tones on. Ruby did evermore love me in a nice pair of shoes. I'll wear the pajamas I got for Christmas a few years ago, still in the plastic, and I'll act normal, like I'm not expecting anything but a good night's sleep in my new pajamas and clean bed. I sure don't need to look like I'm on the lookout for any irregular company. And maybe, just maybe, if I look enough like I'm minding my own business she'll come in again and slip in beside me. I don't know what I'll do then. I wouldn't want to scare her off.

What do you think of the odds? They say good things will happen when you least expect it and what goes around comes around and so forth. I just hope that's so. But if something happens and she doesn't show up, it won't be the end of the world. She's been here once, I'm sure.

And I'll tell you, having your dead wife haint you can

really tip your day off to a fine start. Outside I've got the sheets flapping in the wind, I had the coffee turn out this morning, and I got a free sample of gargle in the mailbox. I think about all I've got left to do is fix up for her and say, "Ruby Pitt Woodrow Stokes! Come on down!"

16.

For every minute Jack slept that night he was awake for two. Every branch scraping the roof was Ruby descending, every dog scrambling underneath the porch was Ruby rising. Only when he woke up at daylight and released himself from his damp, tangled sheets did he realize that his own body had fooled his heart the night before, just as trees and dogs had caused him to lie and wait. And sleeping and awake he had dreamt of Ruby. He needed relief from his night, but holding her pillow and crying as he'd done other nights would not help him. His frustration and anger had rooted in and taken hold well below the place where tears start, and so would not be washed up nor out by them. His pain was the sort that burrows in and tortures until the source of the struggle is understood, reconciled, and removed.

So little to you, foolish old man, you invent something, then get mad when what you thought was so ain't so. Woke up wound around a thousand nights, pull the sheet out from the foot of the bed and it'll wind around you, then wake up one night and call it Ruby, me laying on the sheet and calling for Ruby. No fool like a goddamn old fool. It's what I get for wanting something. All I want me now is a drink of liquor, wanting to take a drink. Goddamn room smelling like babies, damn dusting powder in the sheets. Air it out then! Stood up by a haint, what I mean to tell you, and not even stood up by one real.

He got out of bed and opened a window. The view to Burr's house was obscured by a lush thickness of flowering trees. He didn't see June's car there, or June on the porch with her father, hearing about Mavis, laughing some, then remembering Ruby. *I wish she'd been my mother. I wish she hadn't died.*

He left the window open and walked outside to the pony shelter to retrieve his liquor bottle. Today would be the first time since he married Ruby that there would be a bottle in the house. *King of my goddamn castle now, by God. Somebody passing by sees my pajamas, let them look. Take a picture! It'll last longer!* He was glad he'd worn his shoes, dew was still on the grass. He thought how the shoes would've made Ruby laugh. *You do tickle me, always up to something.*

He stopped in the yard and looked at the woods across the field. He didn't want to think about her anymore, her leaving, her not coming back, especially her leaving. *You laying there in the pink dress June bought, my insides they yelled out, No! God, you were a beautiful woman to me. I'd told June to take the money and go the best place there was and buy the best thing they had, something the color I'd married you in. I couldn't let you go in the wedding dress. I wanted that here to look at it. Burr gave me the money to buy you that one, bless him, and took us to the courthouse, bless him again. And when we put you in the ground, I told mama to accept you next to her, you were a good woman, never meant anybody any harm, neither one, just ways different, that's all, and Burr told me my mama and my daddy and this earth would accept you because your grace was something no one could turn away, and I cried then, Ruby, I cried all the way home.*

June told her father that when she finished cleaning Jack's house she'd like to go back into town and buy some things for supper and they could all eat together. *Something Jack would like, the way Ruby would've made it. She showed me how to make the dough, and we sat at the table, rolled it out and cut it into long strips. Then she held me over the pot and let me drop them in, couldn't tell mama. She had enough evidence against Ruby. Maybe she's happy now, shed of us all, but Roland. Those two. I'm bound to run into her, probably shopping one day, spending daddy's money. I can't believe he supports her. She could work. But I guess the checks keep her happy, no telling how much she socks away for Roland. No, Shelbourne's certainly not big enough for me and my mama. God, I'll walk into the firm one day and she'll be sitting at my desk, tapping a big switch on her knee, saying she'd forgotten to give it to me the time I made Ruby a Mother's Day card, ignored her, or when I started the flower seeds Ruby'd given me in the side yard. Last week, Mr. Johnson, Someone's been waiting to see you, June, I told her to go on in. A woman? Yes. Know her? No. I didn't want to open the door. Not that time, but another. Daddy says if I'm that worried I should move, he'd never tell her where, if she asked. But he's so close out here. I can't. This is my home.*

Jack came back inside, paused in the kitchen, wondering if he should rinse a glass, but he decided to drink from the bottle, matched his mood. Then he pushed the bottle into the waist of his pajama pants, went into the living room, unplugged the television, draped the cord over his shoulder, and began slowly and carefully wheeling the cart down the hall as one would wheel a patient into surgery. *Drink me a little liquor, watch the cartoons, watch them all day if I goddamn feel like it, that's the cure, nobody to stop me. Yes, it's a plenty of ways to stay out from under a woman, stay drunk, stay in front of the television, neither way you don't think, don't feel nothing. These goddamn sheets got to go, shoes, too, silliness.*

He stopped the cart beside the foot of the bed, but before he plugged it in he stripped the bed, took off his shoes, put the sheets in the bottom of the closet and dropped his shoes in on top of them. Then he plugged in the television, flipped channels until he found a very busy, bright cartoon, set the liquor bottle on the nightstand and made himself comfortable on the mattress. He reached over for the bottle, unscrewed the cap, took the longest pull he could stand. *Aaaa, goddamn. Won't take long like that. Look. Coyote'll drop a atom bomb on that roadrunner, then that little fool pops up and goes Beep-Beep!* He admired the roadrunner's resiliency, and after its next escapade he had another long drink, then another. His distractions were working, but not quickly enough. Thoughts of Ruby, full and boundless as they were, would not be displaced by the colors, sounds, fresh air, or drunkenness he had brought into her room, and that frustrated him. *What do I have to do?*

He didn't hear Burr's car outside, nor the car doors slamming, nor Burr knocking at the back door.

June told him to go on in, Jack might be napping. They went into the kitchen. June walked straight to the pantry, got out Ruby's apron and tied it around her waist and collected the dirty dishes into the sink. Burr called out, "You in here?" And when he got no answer, the same dread passed through him as when he'd called out that same question in his mother-in-law's home years before. *Beside her bed, robe open, must've happened getting dressed. God, it was awful. To be sure not Jack. No, here's here. But he should've met us at the door, always has.* "Jack, you decent? I've got June with me." June smiled at that and ran the sink full of soapy water.

Oh shit. Me in this liquory powder-smelling mess. Burr'll think I lost my mind. See, if you'd got drunker sooner you'd be passed out now. What am I supposed to do? He's bound to come in, and got June with him. He decided to feign sleep. So with the television still going and the uncapped bottle on the nightstand, Jack rolled over on his side, facing Ruby's place, and started to snore.

Burr followed the cartoon sounds down the hall, knowing something was wrong and feeling it would be up to him to face and fix whatever he was walking into. *He should've met us at the door. The television goes in the living room. Something's bad wrong.*

He pushed open the door and saw the scene Jack had set for himself, heard him snoring over a commercial jingle.

He turned the television off and closed the window, flies were getting in the room. *He's bound to be drunk, picked up that bottle for him, just got it for him yesterday.*

The liquor that was meant to relax him was now making him nauseous. *What am I going to say?* He maintained his rhythmic snoring, counting off the beats, while Burr noticed everything that was strange and out of place about the room, especially the odor. He walked over to the bed, shook Jack's shoulder and said, "Wake up! You drunk? What's going on in here?"

Jack decided to act nonchalant as long as it'd work, then he'd decide what to do next. So he rolled over onto his back, yawned, rubbed his eyes and acted very surprised to see he had company.

"What you doing here?"

"I told you I was bringing June this weekend. What's going on?" Burr measured his tone. Jack Stokes on the defensive was no good, impossible to handle.

"I just wanted to lay up awhile." Jack fluffed the pillows, arranged them, and sat up against them, wishing he'd thought to slide the bottle under the bed. "Sit down and take a load off. Yeah, I forgot about June coming. I hate she had to walk in on a mess in there."

"Looks like the mess is back here," Burr said as he sat down on the edge of the bed. *Why're the sheets piled in the closet? To be sure he didn't mess himself up, no, to be sure not.*

"Well, I just haven't got around to doing anything." Jack squirmed against the pillows.

"Except drinking half a pint of bourbon." *Well, that's it. That'll piss him off sure enough. Now you'll never get a straight answer.*

Smart-ass, how many times did I take you under that pony shelter with me and let you take a drink when Tiny Fran was giving you hell? I'd say, Pour some of this on them bitch bites. "You got something against somebody drinking in his own house? Act like you never seen me take a drink."

"I've never known you to in the house."

Well, he can get it good as Cecil got it, come messing. Everybody ought to leave me alone. Jack felt himself ready to say things he neither meant nor believed. "Well, I guess you don't know me too good, do you?"

"It's not a matter of knowing you or not knowing you, I just know it's not something you'd ordinarily do." Burr hoped that sounded firm but inoffensive. He needed the truth so he could help. He didn't want to be lied to.

Jack didn't know how to reply and not have the conversation continue its circle around the truth he was hiding. "This ain't a ordinary day, so you just go on back home, and you can tell June I'm back here resting and she can skip this room. I'll clean it up sometime directly."

"But what you're really going to do is lay back here on this bare mattress and drink liquor and watch television all day."

"I will if I've a mind to." *Why don't he just go on?*

"Well, I'll tell June just to come pick up the wash out of here. She can run a load, the sheets over there, while she's here."

Powders in them. "Don't nobody touch the sheets! I'll take care of the sheets!" Jack started off the mattress and headed for the closet. He didn't know what he'd do with the sheets once he had them, but he didn't want June saying, "His sheets smell funny, daddy, they smell like lilacs, look at the powder fogging out of them." Then Burr would really want to know something.

Burr sat and watched Jack, amazed. *He's clean, so he didn't have an accident. What's he doing?* Jack rolled the shoes up in the sheets, grabbed the bundle up, and held it tightly as he crawled back onto the mattress.

"Are you out of your mind, Jack? Now I want to know what's going on. I know you're half lit, but this is pure craziness!"

He's not getting my sheets. "All that work you need to do, to be sure you can find something to do besides bother somebody about his laundry. This is my business. You better go tend to yours."

Perfume. There's perfume on them. "What's that smell?"

"What smell?" *It's your upper lip. Wishing for something,*

see if I do again. He knew he was doing a poor job keeping Burr back. His defiance was not working for him but against him. He crammed the bundle between his legs and hoped that that would be adequate in keeping more lilac scent from wafting towards Burr.

June washed all the dishes, swept the floor and wiped down the cabinets. Before cleaning the next room she decided to check on Jack, so she dried her hands on Ruby's apron and walked down the hall.

"I asked you, what's that odor?" *I might as well be talking to Roland. That's exactly how he'd look at me, holding money he'd taken out of my wallet, hiding it behind his back, I know you took it, now give it to me, and he'd stare me right in the eyes like I was an idiot for thinking so.*

You want to know? It's lilac dusting powder. You want to know what else? I put it all on these sheets last night, thinking she'd like it. I bet you'd have loved to've seen me in here sprinkling like a goddamn fool. And you know why? I honest to God believed she was coming back to me. Now shut up. Jack was forming his answer when June walked in. *God, that's a pretty thing in Ruby's apron.*

June knew she'd walked in on the middle of something. She trusted that her father was finding out exactly what. *I love those two. Fix this, daddy, something's wrong with Jack, fix it.*

Burr looked up at June and said, "Baby, Jack's about to tell me why his sheets smell like gardenia blossoms."

Don't take that tone with him, daddy. You'll never get anywhere with him. Remember how Ruby'd have to handle him sometimes? You know him. Talk to him like you do.

Jack was happy to see June, and he wished he weren't in the middle of this tussle with her father or he'd tell her so. He decided to talk with her when this was over, when he found a way to make Burr back down. But he had to finish this first.

"And I was just telling your daddy here he ought to go on and leave me back here, let you clean the front, everybody mind his own business." *Now I got two sniffing around. And it is not gardenia blossoms!*

Burr wanted the truth. "June, go ahead and throw those sheets there in the washer, and I'll bet they'd dry outside in no time." And when she started for the bed, Jack jerked the bundle up into his chest and screamed out, "I told you to leave the goddamn sheets be! It's all I and Ruby's business, but you're bound and determined to know something. Well, I fixed them for her. Last night I made things ready for her. I thought she was coming home to me. You satisfied? That make you happy?"

Neither Burr nor June had heard that voice or seen that face before, and they were stunned by the force of his words. Pulling his knees up to his chest, he cradled the sheets, pressed his face into them and began to cry. *I told him to leave me alone. It's all mine and Ruby's business. I told him to go.*

June sat down beside Jack and rubbed the back of his neck. *It's okay. We all miss her. It's okay.* "You can talk to us, Jack. You talk to us if you need to. Daddy didn't mean any harm. He didn't know."

Jack spoke half to himself, half to them, words muffled in the sheets, "Nothing to say. I'll be all right. Started out with nothing, ending up with nothing. Just go on home and leave me be." *Made do with nothing when mama and daddy died too, not like I don't know how, don't want to though. I want Ruby. That'd cure me. Why am I in this bed? Never been sick or sorry enough to do this. I've got to get up, embarrassing. Ruby'd say when you don't feel like you want to get up and go and do, that's when you've got to make yourself, one foot in front of the other. I better sober up first.*

Why'd I have to push Jack? Why didn't I just let it go? Satisfying your own goddamn curiosity. Couldn't you tell? This is not my business, give him credit for having some. Give him credit, for God's sakes, for being a man. Without saying a word, Burr looked at his daughter and asked what he should do.

I don't know, daddy. Maybe that's not the right question.

Just help him. You've known him all this time, you must know what he needs.

Burr looked at Jack, hunched over the sheets, arms around his knees. *He needed his mother, and she died. He needed Ruby, she also died. He needed children and a place of his own, he never had them. I can't raise the dead, but I have shared my child with him, with Ruby. I do have land. I've always thought of this place as his, and hasn't he known that? Whether he has or he hasn't, it doesn't matter, it's not his. What else can he have now?*

Burr moved up on the bed, closer to Jack. *I'll do this for him now.* June kept her hand on Jack's head, rubbing his hair, soothing him. She looked at her father and felt that this bad time would soon be over.

"Jack, I want you to listen to me." June heard her father and rested her hand on Jack's shoulder.

What can Burr say? He can't say Ruby's got the coffee on, can't say she wants me to bridle the mule for her. What can he say, except "Do the best you can."

Burr looked at his daughter's hand on Jack's shoulder and said, "I'm giving you this piece of land, Jack. We'll go outside and you can walk off what you want. It's always been yours, you worked it, but now I want you to have it outright." *There, it's said.*

Jack lifted his head, looked first at June then her father

and then out the open window at the field and the woods beyond the field. *He wants to give that to you. It could belong to you, you know how you've wanted this place, don't be proud now, you take it, you take it and work it with the time that's left to you. Ruby'd say to take it, do it and be glad for it, if that's what you want, otherwise leave it alone, but you know you want it. I want her more, but do I refuse one because I can't have the other? No, I don't think so. And it won't replace her, I know that. I'll just have something of my own, keep me from going out of here the way I came in. I will have it. I think I will. And now, let me try to live.*